Caribbean Revolutions

This book provides both a should be an historical introduction and a comparative analysis of the five most important guerrilla movements in the Caribbean Basin between 1959 and the 1990s, including Guatemala, El Salvador, Nicaragua, Colombia, and Puerto Rico. The authors argue that the Cold War shaped and fueled the structure, tactics, and ideologies of the diverse revolutionary movements in the region. The authors also address the particular impact that the Cuban Revolution had on the region. The first chapter of *Caribbean Revolutions* provides an introduction to the Cuban Revolution, the Cold War, and Marxist thought. Succeeding chapters analyze each case study individually and also provide discussions on the current political situation for all of the organizations covered in the book that remain active. With lists of suggested reading and extra resources in each chapter, this is written as an accessible course book for students of Latin American history and politics.

Rachel A. May is Director of the Institute for the Study of Latin America and the Caribbean (ISLAC) at the University of South Florida. She is the author of *Terror in the Countryside: Campesino Responses to Political Violence in Guatemala, 1954–1985* (2001). She is the coeditor and a contributor to *(Un)Civil Societies: Human Rights and Democratic Transitions in Eastern Europe and Latin America* (2007) and *La Florida: Five Hundred Years of Hispanic Presence* (2014).

Alejandro Schneider is Professor of History at both the University of Buenos Aires and the National University of La Plata (Argentina). He is a labor historian who has worked on the history of armed and social movements in Latin America, and he is the author or editor of fourteen books on Argentine and Latin American history.

Roberto González Arana is Professor of History and Director of the Institute of Latin America and the Caribbean Studies at the University of the North (UniNorte) in Barranquilla, Colombia. His many publications include *Dictaduras en el Caribe* (2018) and *Sociedades en Conflicto: movimientos sociales en América Latina* (2016).

Caribbean Revolutions

Cold War Armed Movements

RACHEL A. MAY

University of South Florida

ALEJANDRO SCHNEIDER

*University of Buenos Aires and the National University
of La Plata (Argentina)*

ROBERTO GONZÁLEZ ARANA

University of the North (UniNorte), Colombia

CAMBRIDGE
UNIVERSITY PRESS

CAMBRIDGE
UNIVERSITY PRESS

University Printing House, Cambridge CB2 8BS, United Kingdom

One Liberty Plaza, 20th Floor, New York, NY 10006, USA

477 Williamstown Road, Port Melbourne, VIC 3207, Australia

314–321, 3rd Floor, Plot 3, Splendor Forum, Jasola District Centre, New Delhi – 110025, India

79 Anson Road, #06–04/06, Singapore 079906

Cambridge University Press is part of the University of Cambridge.

It furthers the University's mission by disseminating knowledge in the pursuit of education, learning, and research at the highest international levels of excellence.

www.cambridge.org
Information on this title: www.cambridge.org/9781108424752
DOI: 10.1017/9781108344081

First published 2018

Printed in the United States of America by Sheridan Books, Inc.

A catalogue record for this publication is available from the British Library.

ISBN 978-1-108-42475-2 Hardback
ISBN 978-1-108-44090-5 Paperback

Contents

Figures

Acknowledgments

This book was several years in the making, but we hope it is better for these extended efforts. The three of us met for the first time in Barranquilla several years ago, thanks to invitations from the Universidad del Norte. We started this project as a workshop for graduate students from the University of South Florida (USF) only a few months after that first meeting. For their sponsorship of that workshop, we would like to thank the staff of the Institute for the Study of Latin America and the Caribbean (ISLAC) at USF. We would also like to thank Timothy Wickham Crowley, who was the discussant at our 2014 LASA panel on armed revolutionary movements in the Caribbean. His commentary was thorough and thoughtful; as a result, we were inspired to continue with the book. Deborah Gershenowitz has encouraged us along the way. Both her input and her patience were invaluable. And of course we are most grateful to our partners and families, especially Doug Dusini, Ivonne Molinares, and Victoria Ugartemendia.

Acronyms

AD-M-19	*Alianza Democrática*
ANAPO	*Alianza Nacional Popular*
ANC	*Acción Nacional Conservadora*
ATC	*Asociación de Trabajadores del Campo*
BPP	*Bloque Popular Patriótico*
BPR	*Bloque Popular Revolucionario*
CAL	*Comandos Armados de Liberación*
CDC	*Comitésde Defensa Civil*
CEBs	*Comunidades Eclesiales de Base*
CGCS	*Coordinadora Guerrillera Simón Bolívar*
CGT-I	*Confederación General de Trabajadores Independientes*
CNG	*Coordinadora Nacional Guerrillera*
CNR	*Comisión Nacional de Reconciliación*
COSEP	*Consejo Superior de la Empresa Privada*
CRM	*Coordinación Revolucionaria de las Masas*
CTC	*Confederación de Trabajadores Colombianos*
CTN	*Confederación de Trabajadores Nicaragüenses.*
CUUN	*Centro Universitario de la Universidad Nacional*
DRU	*Dirección Revolucionaria Unida*
EDSNN	*Ejército Defensor de la Soberanía Nacionalde Nicaragua*
EGP	*Ejército Guerrillero de los Pobres*
ELN	*Ejércitode Liberación Nacional*
EPR	*Ejército Revolucionario Popular*
ERP	*Ejército Revolucionario del Pueblo*
ERTC	*Ejército Revolucionario de los Trabajadores Centroamericanos*

EZLN	*Ejército Zapatista de Liberación Nacional*
FAL	*Fuerzas Armadas para la Liberación*
FALN	*Fuerzas Armadas de Liberación Nacional*
FAO	*Frente Amplio Opositor*
FAR	*Fuerzas Armadas Rebeldes*
FARC	*Fuerzas Armadas Revolucionarias de Colombia*
FARC- EP	*Fuerzas Armadas Revolucionarias de Colombia–Ejército Popular*
FARN	*Fuerzas Armadas de Resistencia Nacional*
FARP	*Fuerzas Armadas de Resistencia Popular*
FDR	*Frente Democrático Revolucionario*
FER	*Frente de Estudiantes Revolucionarios*
FGEI	*Frente Guerrillero Edgar Ibarra*
FLN	*Frente de Liberación Nacional*
FMLN	*Frente Farabundo Martí para la Liberación Nacional*
FPL	*Fuerzas Populares de Liberación*
FPN	*Frente Patriótico Nacional*
FRS	*Frente Revolucionario Sandino*
FSLN	*Frente Sandinista de Liberación Nacional*
FUAR	*Frente Unida de Acción Revoucionaria*
FUN	*Federación Universitaria Nacional*
FUR	*Frente Unida de Resistencia.*
GPP	*Guerra Prolongada Popular*
JMRL	*Juventudes del Movimiento Revolucionario Liberal*
JRN	*Juventud Revolucionaria Nicaragüense*
M-19	*Movimiento 19 de Abril*
MAP	*Movimiento Armado del Pueblo*
MCR	*Movimiento Cristiano Revolucionario*
MES	*Movimiento Estudiantil de Secundaria*
MIRA	*Movimiento Independentista Revolucionario en Armas*
MLC	*Movimiento Liberal Constitucionalista*
MLP	*Movimiento de Liberación del Pueblo*
MNN	*Movimiento Nueva Nicaragua*
MOEC	*Movimiento Obrero Estudiantil Campesino*
MPI	*Movimiento Pro Independencia*
MPU	*Movimiento Pueblo Unido*
MR-13	*Movimiento Rebelde 13 de Noviembre*
MRL	*Movimiento Revolucionario Liberal*
ORPA	*Organización Revolucionaria del Pueblo en Armas*
ORT	*Organización Revolucionaria de Trabajadores*

OSPAAAL	*Organización de Solidaridad con Asia, África y América Latina*
OVRP	*Organización de Voluntarios Por la Revolución Puertorriqueña*
PCC	*Partido Comunista Colombiano*
PCS	*Partido Comunista de El Salvador*
PDC	*Partido dela Democracia Cristiana*
PGT	*Partido Guatemalteco del Trabajo*
PIP	*Partido Independentista Puertorriqueño*
PLI	*Partido Liberal Independiente*
PPSC	*Partido Popular Social Cristiano*
PRT	*Partido Revolucionario de Trabajadores*
PRTC	*Partido Revolucionario de Trabajadores de Centroamérica*
PRTP-EPB	*Partido Revolucionario de los Trabajadores Puertorriqueños Ejército Popular Boricua*
PSC	*Partido Social Cristiano*
PSdeN	*Partido Socialista de Nicaragua*
PSN	*Partido Socialista Nicaragüense*
PSP	*Partido Socialista Puertorriqueño*
RN	*Resistencia Nacional*
TP	*Tendencia Proletariado*
UDEL	*Unión Democrática de Liberación*
UDN	*Unión Democrática Nacionalista*
UJCC	*Unión de Juventudes Comunistas de Colombia*
UNAN	*Universidad Nacional Autónoma de Nicaragua*
UP	*Unión Patriótica*
URNG	*Unidad Revolucionaria Nacional de Guatemala*

Cuban Revolutionaries and the Caribbean Basin: An Introduction

It is hard to overstate the impact of Fidel Castro's 26th of July Movement's triumphant march into Havana in January 1959. The Cuban Revolution – launched less than three years earlier by a small group of young social activists with virtually no military experience – created a sense of optimism and possibility throughout the world. The exhilaration and hope that emanated from this military victory had an impact everywhere, but the way this Revolution would dramatically alter the course of history in its own neighborhood is the subject here. Within a few years there were armed revolutionary movements in virtually every country in Latin America and the Caribbean (and also in many other countries and regions, including the United States) that were modeling their attempts at radical societal transformation on Che Guevara's *foquismo*.

Foquismo or "foco theory" is the name given to the revolutionary strategy of Ernesto "Che" Guevara, who proposed that revolutionary activists should move to immediately launch a guerrilla war on regular armies in countries with high levels of rural poverty and repressive states. The foco theory makes the claim that revolutionary guerrillas could successfully leverage their strategic advantages by appealing to oppressed *campesinos*,[1] and carrying out acts of sabotage on regular armies in remote regions of poor countries where regular armies would be unfamiliar with the terrain. These foquista movements – with their multitude of

[1] Campesinos are poor people who are engaged in agricultural work. This Spanish term literally means "rural dweller," but it only applies to men and women who are poor, and of low social status.

origins – evolved over decades in much of the Caribbean. This challenge to traditional elites and US hegemony eventually led to state terrorism in much of the region, and outright civil war in a few cases. These conflicts – especially the Caribbean revolutions – to a large extent defined the Cold War in this hemisphere. Without understanding these diverse armed revolutionary movements, we cannot fully understand social movements or even national politics in Latin America today. The generation that took up arms to challenge social injustice in the decades after the Cuban Revolution is *the* generation that is most represented in the political power structure today. New Social Movements have embraced the iconic representations of their revolutionary predecessors and have defined new militancies in relation to their parents' generation. We are now at the stage of history when it is important to revisit the history of armed struggle in the Caribbean Basin during the Cold War. Many of the social problems and inequalities that inspired these movements have persisted into the present. Guerrilla movements have made or are making the transition to democratic political parties, and many former revolutionaries now carry significant influence in the region. To understand and evaluate the "Left" in Latin America today, we must understand its origins and early experiences.

THE CARIBBEAN BASIN

Defining the "Caribbean" as a bounded geopolitical region can be a complicated and fraught endeavor. Typically the Caribbean is described in terms of geographical, historical, and cultural patterns, but the contours of these boundaries are fluid. For the purposes of this book we are looking at the islands of the Caribbean, along with Central America and the South American countries with Caribbean coastlines that share a common Spanish colonial past, as well as a defined Hispano-Caribbean culture. The case studies included in this volume are Cuba, Guatemala, El Salvador, Nicaragua, Colombia, and Puerto Rico. This does not include every country that had an armed revolutionary insurgency in the region. Most notably we have excluded Mexico and Venezuela. These are two of the largest countries in the region, but they both had relatively minor armed revolutionary movements during this time.

One of the reasons why Mexico had relatively less significant Cold War–era armed movements is that the Mexican Revolution predates the Cold War by one generation. The Mexican Revolution, which began as a popular armed uprising in 1910 was fought for more than a decade and was one of the bloodiest civil conflicts in the region's history. More than 1 million people died during the armed phase of the Mexican Revolution, and many more were forcibly displaced by the conflict. The Mexican Revolution eventually resulted in a very progressive constitution (1917), and some redistribution of wealth and power. So by the mid-1950s, Mexicans already had some of the concessions that Cold War revolutionaries were fighting for elsewhere, and there was also a level of "war fatigue" that still impacted Mexican politics. Despite this, several less impactful armed movements occurred in Mexico during the Cold War, and the Mexican ("revolutionary") government violently repressed social justice activists on several occasions.[2] Nevertheless, the Mexican case is still quite distinct from the other cases here.

This region has historically been a crossroads of international geopolitical competition. It became a focal point of the "hot" manifestations of the Cold War after the Cuban Revolution of 1959.

Spanish Colonialism in the Caribbean

The Caribbean Basin was the center point for European competition and war for the better part of the Spanish colonial era. Because it was the central gateway to all of the Americas, control over this region was strategically and economically key. This set up the Caribbean as the physical space for intense military and economic competition among the European powers between the sixteenth and nineteenth centuries. Consequently Spain was forced to cede control of several possessions in the region, and the enduring influence of British, Dutch, and French colonialism can still be felt today, primarily in the legacy of African slavery.

The Caribbean Basin held comparatively less mineral wealth, and its strategic and military importance made it economically distinct from the rest of Spanish America. African slaves were used to build an agricultural

---

[2] The most notable example of this was the massacre at the Tlatelolco "Plaza de las Tres Culturas." On October 2, 1968, thousands of high school and college students converged on the plaza in Mexico City to protest. While they were peacefully assembled listening to a series of political speeches by activists, the Mexican armed forces opened fire on the protesters. Between 300 and 400 people were shot, and more than 1,000 were arrested. The massacre occurred just ten days before the opening of the Olympics, and it is believed that the Mexican government feared embarrassment by social mobilization and protest in front of the international press corps.

basis for colonization in the region, and Caribbean ports became the hub of the Atlantic slave trade.

The complex legacy of the Caribbean as a military outpost and a central nucleus of the slave trade ensured that the region had more geopolitical significance than one might expect, and it also established a precedent for brutality and exploitation that is not insignificant.

Independence and the Modern Era in the Caribbean

The Caribbean Basin was the first part of the Americas to be colonized by Spain, and Spanish colonization lasted until almost the end of the nineteenth century for most of the region as well (and other European colonies endured well into the middle of the twentieth century). This meant that most of this region was colonized for at least 100 years longer than anywhere else in the Americas. When independence did finally come to the Spanish Caribbean islands, it was only after the United States entered the Spanish-American War. Consequently one form of colonization was essentially replaced with another. Although the mainland Caribbean countries of Central and South America did not endure the humiliation of official US protectionism, they were subject to a similar US worldview, which resulted in frequent US intervention, including direct military intervention and occupation in some cases.

The United States acknowledged the geopolitical unity of the Caribbean Basin in the context of the Cold War with Ronald Reagan's Caribbean Basin Initiative (CBI) in the 1980s. The CBI was designed to give preferential tariffs and terms of trade to Caribbean countries (including Central and South American countries with Caribbean coastlines) that were openly anti-communist and explicitly aligned with US interests in the Cold War. To further these aims, Ronald Reagan signed into law the Caribbean Basin Economic Recovery Act in August 1983. The CBI defined the region being examined here in geopolitical terms, and it was an acknowledgment of the US perspective on the primacy of the region's strategic importance in the Cold War.

THE CUBAN REVOLUTION

Why Cuba?

Cuba's history is in many ways unique in Latin America. It was among the first places in the New World to be colonized by the Spanish. The first permanent Spanish settlement was established in what is today Havana by 1514. The island served as a laboratory for colonization in the Americas, often experiencing the worst of Spanish conquest and governance before these strategies and policies were abandoned for more reasonable and less destructive tactics elsewhere. There was little mineral wealth but the large island colony was always of primary strategic and military importance in the contested terrain of the Caribbean. Cuba was large enough to make both agriculture and African slavery profitable. In many ways it was the front door to the New World, and it was protected with a ferocity that was unparalleled in the Spanish Empire.

The Haitian slave rebellion and Revolution (1791–1804) provided an impetus for a rapid expansion of the slave trade in Cuba, as the plantation economy (and the slave trade) collapsed in neighboring Hispaniola (today Haiti and the Dominican Republic). The Cuban colony experienced a large influx of slaves, which accompanied the increased profitability of slave trading and sugar production that resulted from the decline in regional competition. It is notable that Cuba experienced growth in slave trading and an increase in the Afro-descendant population at precisely the same time that the slave trade was in decline elsewhere. In addition the Haitian Revolution, and the slave uprising that it evoked, made independence from Spain unattractive to Spanish Creole elites in the early nineteenth century. Consequently Cuba's independence from Spain was delayed for almost a full century after the rest of the empire had collapsed. Cuba, therefore, had a much longer period of direct colonial rule than anywhere else in the Americas.

José Martí – an important contributor to the intellectual canon of Latin America – promulgated a revolutionary independence movement in 1895 (which was ironically planned and funded from Martí's exile in the United States), but he was martyred in the early days of fighting. The first Cuban Revolution was then effectively hijacked by the United States in 1898. After three years of heavy fighting, the United States declared war on Spain and entered Cuba with a fair amount of Cuban support. The alliance between Cuban and American forces meant quick victory over the Spanish after only ten weeks. Subsequently the United States negotiated a peace with Spain (the Treaty of Paris) that did not include Cuban negotiators and did not consider Cuban nationalist interests. The United States took several Spanish colonies (e.g., Puerto Rico and Guam) and established Cuba as a "protectorate." Hopes for Cuban independence dimmed after the United States included the Platt Amendment in the new Cuban Constitution in 1902, giving the United

States the right to intervene militarily in the island nation whenever US interests were deemed to be at stake. The US military occupied Cuba between 1898 and 1902, and again between 1906 and 1908. Marines landed again in 1912 and in 1917 to protect US property and interests. Cuban independence was extraordinarily compromised by US economic and political domination of the island. Cuban reliance on sugar (which was refined and sold almost exclusively by American companies) increased dramatically in the first half of the twentieth century. And sugar had (and has) a powerful historical association with colonialism and slavery. By the time of the Cold War, *anti-yanqui* sentiment was peaking in Cuba.

Why Fidel?

Fidel Castro was undoubtedly one of the most influential men of the twentieth century. He was born into an elite land-owning family as the illegitimate child of a wealthy Spanish sugar planter and his household servant. His parents eventually married, and Fidel Castro was baptized and formally recognized by his father when he was eight years old. Castro attended the University of Havana where he studied law and became a student leader, which thrust him onto the national political stage. He was active in the Cuban *Ortodoxo* party and present when the leader of the party, Eddie Chibas, committed suicide in 1951. This dramatic event combined with increasing and overt government corruption created a legitimacy crisis. Political morale was already compromised when Fulgencio Batista staged a military coup in 1952 and canceled scheduled elections. Castro initially tried to use his legal training to force Batista to step down. When these attempts proved unsuccessful, Castro conspired with other disaffected political allies to launch an armed insurrection.

Castro formed a group that attacked the Moncada military barracks on July 26, 1953. The attack was a failure and Castro was arrested soon after and put on trial, where he famously declared to a national audience that "history would absolve [him]." He, along with several other comrades from his movement, now called the "26th of July Movement," were held for almost two years. In 1955 Batista came to believe that an amnesty for the popular political prisoners would bolster his own failing legitimacy. Castro, along with his brother Raul and several other members of the 26th of July Movement were released from prison and left Cuba for Mexico later that year. In Mexico they met other Cuban and Latin American dissidents including Ernesto Che Guevara, an Argentine doctor and political activist. The 26th of July Movement continued to organize and gain followers inside of Cuba, and Castro and the other revolutionaries in Mexico gained some (minimal) training in guerrilla warfare, raised funds, and worked on building connections with other dissident groups inside Cuba.

In December 1956 Castro and his guerrilla foco crash-landed their yacht, *The Granma*, in a mangrove swamp. Batista's troops were waiting for them, and only nineteen of the original eighty-two guerrilla fighters survived the ambush by the Cuban National Guard. From the nearby Sierra Maestra, this small guerrilla foco launched its guerrilla offensive by recruiting new members within the poorest and most remote regions of the country.

Guerrilla Warfare

The strategy of the guerrilla foco was both pragmatic and novel. Although Guevara was well versed in Marxist/Leninist/Maoist theory and strategy, the Cuban revolutionaries forged their own path and never sought direction from the Cuban Communist Party or the Soviet Union. Guevara was both the intellectual and the scribe for the Revolution, but most historians believe that the strategy of guerrilla warfare (or foquismo) was developed in concert between Fidel and Che, as he became known.[3] According to Guevara in the widely published revolutionary manual *Guerrilla Warfare*, the "fundamental lessons" of the Cuban military-revolutionary experience were

(1) Popular forces can win a war against the army.
(2) It is not necessary to wait until all conditions for making revolution exist; the insurrection can create them.
(3) In underdeveloped America, the countryside is the ideal theater for armed insurrection.[4]

Guevara believed and promoted the idea that there was only one necessary objective precondition for revolution, and this was absolute poverty (*miseria*). And there was one necessary subjective precondition – that

---

[3] "Che" is a common term of endearment or familiarity used between Argentines, particularly boys and men – it is akin to "buddy" or "man." Because Guevara used this term (which is not commonly used outside of Argentina), he became known among his Cuban comrades as "Che" or "El Che."

[4] Che Guevara, *Guerrilla Warfare* (Lincoln: University of Nebraska Press, 1985), 47.

was, absolute faith in the first lesson of the Cuban Revolution – victory (of the "popular forces" over the conventional army) is possible or even inevitable. Guevara also promoted the idea of a continental revolution in Latin America. He believed that pervasive poverty and injustice combined with US imperialism provided the perfect conditions for a revolution in all of Latin America.

The most important element of foquismo was the idea that the popular will for revolution could be created *by* a popular insurrection. This eliminated the need for potential revolutionaries to organize a revolutionary vanguard, or even to do massive peasant or worker organization and education campaigns. Guevara believed that a small guerrilla foco (nineteen combatants in the case of Cuba) would be sufficient to ignite a widespread insurrection through acts of sabotage and provocation. This foco would eventually (and inevitably) grow into a regular army capable of defeating the forces of oppression.

What this meant for social activists in other poor and less developed countries, particularly and explicitly the other countries of Latin America and the Caribbean, was that revolutionary armed struggle could be initiated immediately. And indeed especially after the publication of *Guerrilla Warfare* in 1960, this is what happened.

Unfortunately for the cause of social revolution, counterrevolutionary forces (including the US military) also read *Guerrilla Warfare* and the Cuban experience was never repeated. Moreover a certain mythology behind the idea of foquismo belied the reality of Cuba in the 1950s. In addition to Castro's foco, an organized resistance was already formed within the urban areas of Cuba before the landing of the *Granma*. The 26th of July Movement *did* have a well-organized base of support before it initiated its guerrilla strategy. And this organized popular opposition was able to support the guerrilla movement through real material contributions and substantial logistical assistance. Because the myth of the bearded men in the Sierra Maestra was crucial to the legitimacy of the new revolution, the contributions of an already organized resistance and urban insurrectionists were downplayed in the official propaganda of the Cuban Revolution.

The armed revolutionary movements that were inspired by the mythology of the Cuban Revolution, especially those in the Caribbean Basin, were of extraordinary importance in shaping Cold War politics in the region and in the world. Their stories are full of pathos and their experiences have shaped contemporary politics and provide an important context for understanding New Social Movements and the transitions to democracy that followed the Cold War in Latin America.

THE COLD WAR CONTEXT

Not only did the Cuban Revolution radicalize and inspire the Left, it also radicalized the anti-communist Right, both in Latin America and the United States. The timing was ripe then for this grand social rift, both within Cuban society and within the geopolitical dynamics of the region that became so quickly and neatly a major front of the Cold War.

Castro's ideological convictions in 1959 will perhaps forever be unclear. He (unlike Raul Castro and Che Guevara) had no prior affiliations with the Communist Party or other explicitly Marxist or pro-Soviet groups. He had an established history with liberal democratic politics. But he was certainly not unfamiliar with the whole range of Leftist ideology, and his commitment to social justice based on redistributive policies was also clear.

Castro was careful to be muted in his anti-Yankee sentiment before the 1959 victory, but as soon as he took power he unleashed his brand of extremely anti-American ideological rhetoric. Because of Cuba's neocolonial experience with the United States in the twentieth century, Castro's anti-Americanism was not only sincere but also popular (and pragmatic). His commitment to social justice and redistribution was resonant with a broad base of poor peasants and workers as well as with the middle class. Cuba's reliance on sugar exports and tourism (both controlled by US interests) produced fairly severe economic dislocations, especially among the rural poor and the seasonally unemployed sugar plantation workers. This meant that Castro's (and the Revolution's) anti-imperialist, anti-American sentiment was widely shared, and that redistributive policies were strongly supported by a large cross section of Cuban society. The leaders of Castro's revolutionary government also consolidated their power by arresting and executing opponents who were connected to the Batista regime, the police, and the National Guard, and by targeted repression of opposition elements within Cuban society. He encouraged the mass exodus of "counterrevolutionary" Cubans to Miami.[5]

Fidel very quickly embarked on a massive redistribution campaign, expropriating American-held property as well as the rural landholdings of Cuba's traditional landed elites, including his own properties and those of his family. He also launched a nationwide literacy campaign and reformed the Cuban educational system in a way that was explicitly

---

[5] Castro called the political and class enemies of the Revolution *gusanos* or "worms." He argued that they would have to leave to avoid the contamination of the Revolution.

designed to propagandize his own revolutionary message. All of this created a strong populist base of support for the Revolution, and it also alienated many in Cuba as well as in the United States. The United States broke off diplomatic relations in January 1961.

Between April 17 and April 19, 1961, the CIA trained and funded an army of Cuban exiles who invaded Cuba (at the Bay of Pigs) and unsuccessfully attempted to overthrow the popular Revolutionary government. The invading force surrendered on April 20. Most of the troops were tried in Cuba and then sent back to the United States.

In October 1962, a thirteen-day standoff between the Soviet Union and President John F. Kennedy's White House resulted in the Soviet Union's promise to withdraw its planned nuclear missile arsenal for Cuba, and in return the United States pledged not to launch another military invasion of Cuba (to refrain from attempting to militarily overthrow the Revolution). These tense negotiations between Russian prime minister Nikita Khrushchev and Kennedy placed Cuba, for a time at least, in the center of the Cold War and sealed the fate of the Cuban Revolution as a catalyst. On December 2, 1962, almost two years after the Revolution, Fidel Castro declared that he was a Marxist-Leninist, and that he would be one for the rest of his life.[6]

The explosion of optimism and expanded possibilities after 1959, and especially after the publication of *Guerrilla Warfare* meant that a broad range of populist political coalitions as well as traditional socialist and communist parties were inspired to take up arms in support of Guevara's revolutionary project. This in turn inspired economic elites, militaries, traditional dictators, and the United States to respond to the threat posed by Cuba, especially after the end of the second year.

The United States set out to prevent another Soviet beachhead in its "backyard," by channeling economic and military assistance to US-friendly anti-communist regimes. To some degree the establishment of

---

[6] When Castro made his famous speech in December 1961 declaring himself a Marxist-Leninist, this sparked a largely rhetorical debate among analysts and scholars about Castro's earlier intentions – had he been intentionally obscuring his commitment to communism? Or was he moved toward Marxism (pushed into the arms of the Soviet Union) by his experiences, particularly with regard to the United States, in the two years after the Revolution? While this debate can never be resolved, it does make sense to examine exactly what he said on December 2, 1961. In 1962 a pro-Cuba organization called "Fair Play for Cuba" examined the speech in an eighty-three-page pamphlet (published by Walter Lippmann) to contextualize Castro's bold admission. The pamphlet was scanned and placed on the web. The scanned pamphlet is available at www.walterlippmann.com/fc-12-02-1961.html.

the United States Agency for International Development (USAID), the Peace Corps, and the Alliance for Progress was tacit recognition of the truth of Guevara's thesis – poor and marginalized Latin Americans were highly vulnerable to the Marxist-inspired revolutionary message of the Cold War in the years after the Cuban Revolution. As the rise of armed movements in Central and South America led to a wave of military dictatorships, the United States found itself supporting anti-communist proxy armies to fight these insurgencies. Eventually much of the region was taken over by military dictatorships, which were increasingly brutal in their mission to annihilate the threat of communist subversion. The United States supported these regimes no matter how illegitimate and despotic. The violent Cold War dichotomy had a way of erasing the complex ideological and cultural differences among armed revolutionary movements and the larger popular struggle that stood against the US-backed military dictatorships in the region.

MARXIST IDEOLOGY – A PRIMER

Because of the importance and impact of the Cuban Revolution and the Cold War, virtually every armed social movement in the less-developed world was influenced by Marxist ideology during this era. It is important to remember that despite the utility of Marxist concepts and the example of the Cuban Revolution for other revolutionaries and would-be revolutionaries in the Caribbean, Marxist theory does not account for an armed guerrilla rebellion. Karl Marx was motivated by the severe exploitation of workers that defined early industrial capitalism in Europe, and he was deeply committed to the creation of a socialist labor movement in Europe in the mid-nineteenth century. Nevertheless, Marx believed that advanced industrial capitalism was unsustainable and would eventually collapse from the dislocations that would arise from the severe disarticulation that would occur when the proletarian classes became too impoverished to consume any of the products that they were producing.

Marx did not think that revolutionary movements would occur among peasants in predominantly agrarian societies, and he did not foresee the age of global capital when peripheral societies would support mass consumption by all social classes in the advanced industrial societies. Marx believed that a revolutionary consciousness would develop naturally among proletarianized wage workers in a factory environment. He believed that revolutionary ideology was entirely dependent upon and determined by the working conditions of the proletarian worker.

Therefore for Marx, peasants who were engaged in traditional agriculture would be incapable of embodying or even understanding revolutionary ideology. Still Marxist ideas about capitalism and worker alienation did hold explanatory value for Latin American social activists despite the fact that the majority of the population in every country in Latin America was still engaged in agriculture in the middle of the twentieth century.

The Russian and Chinese Revolutions set the stage for a Latin American Marxist ideology that would be crystalized in the Cuban Revolution and its aftermath. Because the Bolshevik uprising was spearheaded as a Marxist-inspired revolution by Vladimir Lenin in Russia – a country with a poorly developed capitalist economy, still dominated by feudalism and inhabited by peasants who were engaged almost entirely in feudal land-labor arrangements – Lenin was forced to explain why the first Marxist Revolution was taking place in the least developed economy in Europe. He also redefined the role of the peasant class in the revolutionary struggle. To explain the Russian Revolution Lenin developed the theory of capitalist imperialism, which allowed Russian communists to understand their own exploitation in terms of a larger "global" capitalist system. Lenin argued that revolution at the periphery (Russia) would provide the necessary impetus for revolution in the industrialized West. Lenin and the members his Bolshevik party believed that German, British, French, and American proletarians would follow suit and eventually support the Russian revolutionary proletarians. And Lenin also allowed for peasants to be revolutionary allies in a proletarian (workers') revolution. Leon Trotsky expanded the Leninist idea of imperialism and posited (in opposition to Stalin) that there would have to be a worldwide revolutionary movement that could transcend national borders to truly overthrow the global capitalist regime. Latin American revolutionaries, by contrast, saw themselves in nationalist terms in opposition to the industrialized "center" nations. They can be referred to as "national liberation Marxists," although they did not refer to themselves as such.[7]

Lenin's theoretical and historical contributions set the stage for Maoism and the Chinese Revolution. Mao believed that peasants were not just "revolutionary allies" in a proletarian revolution, but rather that peasants were the true revolutionary protagonists. Mao proposed that

---

[7] In addition to the life and thought of Che Guevara, other Latin American Marxists were also influential, including José Carlos Mariátegui, Camilo Torres, Marta Harnecker, and Regis Debray. See the end of this chapter for suggested reading on and by these Marxist theorists.

revolutionary struggle would be prolonged and unending, and that a peasant revolutionary army would embody the ideals of the revolution through perpetual military struggle. This idea of the peasant-based "prolonged people's war" was very influential among Latin American revolutionaries of the Cold War era, including Che Guevara.

Finally, Che Guevara, in explaining the strategy of guerrilla warfare in Cuba was able to posit that the age of worldwide socialist revolution had finally arrived, and it would begin in the most impoverished, isolated, and neglected regions of the world. And he was able to promote his revolutionary ideology as twentieth-century "Marxism-Leninism."

PHASES OF ARMED STRUGGLE

In the 1960s virtually every country in Latin America had some sort of armed revolutionary movement that attempted revolution through foquismo. By the middle of the decade, most of these movements had experienced some degree of failure. In all of the case studies here with the exception of Puerto Rico (Guatemala, El Salvador, Nicaragua, and Colombia), the first wave of armed movements underwent a regrouping effort and then emerged again. In some cases, new organizations were created, and in other cases shifting alliances reflected new strategies and ideologies. In Central America (Guatemala, El Salvador, and Nicaragua), there were eventually strategic alliances and umbrella organizations that brought about an unprecedented degree of national popular solidarity. By the mid-1980s and more urgently after the collapse of the Soviet Union in 1989, most revolutionary movements were forced to consider some kind of negotiated transition to peace. This third transitional period will also be discussed in this volume. In the case of Colombia, the rise of the illicit narcotics trade coincided with the end of the Cold War, and the resulting financial resources garnered from drug trafficking allowed both the guerrillas and the Colombian government to postpone the end of the conflict until recently. The case of Puerto Rico was distinct and only encompasses a single period. Rather than set arbitrary dates, the phases of Cold War revolutionary struggle are determined individually for each case study here.

VARIABLES

While this text seeks to provide an accessible and comprehensive history of armed revolutionary struggle in five Caribbean Basin nations, we also want to provide a basis for comparative analysis across this region.

To compare the case studies, we have undertaken a systematic analysis of structure and alliances, mobilization strategy, and ideology for the organizations in each phase.

All of the movements here were represented by armed insurgent organizations; as such, they have a certain military structure in common. Nevertheless they emerged in different contexts and in different ways. They emerged from political parties and from disaffected military rebellions; they represented student groups and intellectuals, and others had their origins in bourgeois political parties. These structures changed and evolved over time as they transitioned from politics to armed insurgency, and back to politics. Structures continued to change in response to the counterrevolutionary campaigns in their respective countries. Internal structure can be examined with reference to both horizontal substructures (bureaucracy) and vertical substructures (the hierarchical chain of command). This book will analyze the political-military structure of the organizations in each case study and how they shifted and evolved in relation to one another.

Fidel Castro and Che Guevara started a revolution in the Sierra Maestra with nineteen men. They immediately had to consider the question of whom they would recruit for their movement. Their strategy was to mobilize peasants in the poorest, most abandoned and remote parts of the country. The revolutionary leaders in the other case studies here also had to decide *whom* the revolutionaries would be. In some cases they mobilized peasants or workers or students and intellectuals for strictly ideological reasons. There were strategic considerations about geography and ethnic realities. Mobilization strategy is about the way in which movements and organizations attract members and how they involve them in the work of the movement. Decisions must be made about potential membership, and the methods used to recruit members. This book will consider the mobilization strategies of the movements as they evolved in each phase for each case study.

And lastly we will be examining the guiding revolutionary ideology of the movements. Ideology is naturally complex, and it can be overly simplified if it corresponds roughly to an "ism." But at the heart of it, ideology is about world view. Juan Luís Segundo defines ideology as a system of prioritized goals that an organization or movement wishes to achieve, along with the tactics that can be used to achieve those goals.[8] In this case we are limiting our analysis to groups that engaged in armed

---

[8] Juan Luís Segundo. *Faith and Ideologies* (Maryknoll, NY: Orbis Books, 1982), 16.

struggle. This was a decision that had to emanate from ideology, or at the very least had to be made consistent with ideology. The success of the Cuban Revolution made it necessary for many (who might not have otherwise been inclined) to justify the use of a military strategy in terms of their preexisting ideological convictions. These decisions were often contentious and sometimes caused fissures within the movements. And ideologies evolved over time, both within and between the phases. For the purposes of this study, ideology will be defined as a holistic world view and philosophy that inform actions and strategy. In this study we will consider the ideologies of the movements in each of the phases as well.

THE CASE STUDIES

The five Caribbean case studies here had active and impactful armed insurgencies during the decades immediately after the Cuban Revolution (1959). The five nations – Guatemala, El Salvador, Nicaragua, Colombia, and Puerto Rico – share a common geography and a common history and culture. They also have unique stories of highly nationalistic armed rebellion that reflect important differences. Our purpose is to provide a detailed history of armed revolutionary movements in the Caribbean Basin. The case studies are not comprehensive, as every country in the region had some kind of armed rebel uprising in response to Cuba's opening the doors of possibility for revolution. But the five important cases represented here do provide a window into understanding the politics of the entire region, both then and now. They represent different national, economic, and ethnic realities. And in the last case of Puerto Rico, we consider a movement whose struggle for political liberation was actual rather than metaphorical. The movements had varying degrees of military and political success. An analysis of these case studies will allow us to draw new conclusions about what constitutes a "successful" revolutionary movement.

Guatemala

The Guatemalan "Revolution" (1944–1954) was a liberal bourgeois revolution aimed at restoring liberal democracy and supporting reformist redistributive policies that sought to diminish the hegemonic influence of the United Fruit Company and other US interests. The United States, in response to an agrarian reform program that expropriated reserve farmland owned by the United Fruit Company, made an example of Guatemala by funding and training a small force of disaffected military men to overthrow the state. They waged a psychological campaign, using the radio to convince both the Guatemalan army and the civilian government that there was a much larger invading force approaching the capital city. President Jacobo Arbenz fled the country prematurely. Che Guevara was living in Guatemala during the days before the collapse of the Guatemalan government (and also before he had made the acquaintance of Fidel Castro). This event had a radicalizing effect on Guevara and others, who were convinced that redistribution and social justice could not be achieved in the backyard of the United States through peaceful democratic means.

Guatemala's armed revolutionary movement began in 1960. The 1961 Bay of Pigs invasion in Cuba was modeled after the earlier (successful) invasion and overthrow of the reformist government in Guatemala in 1954. The Cuban exiles who invaded Cuba at the Bay of Pigs were actually trained in Guatemala during most of 1960. The specter of revolution in Cuba created nationalist (anti-US) sentiment among a class of lower-ranking Guatemalan military officers, who staged a failed coup in 1960. They escaped to the remote region of Izábal afterward, where (using foquismo as a model) they attempted to launch a revolution. In 1961 the Communist Party in Guatemala (the PGT)[9] also resolved to use "all means of struggle," opening the door to armed revolution.

The organizations that took up arms in the 1960s (inspired by Cuba) were decimated by the Guatemalan military before the end of that decade. When they reemerged in the 1970s, they represented a broader base of political aspirations. The counterrevolutionary response of the Guatemalan military was also much more chaotic and violent in the second decade of counterinsurgency. By the time Efraín Ríos Montt launched his genocidal campaign against the poor indigenous communities of the western highlands in 1982, the revolutionary movements had united and had forged a political alliance with a broad base of the non-violent popular movement. The Guatemalan National Revolutionary Unity (URNG)[10] eventually negotiated a series of peace accords with the Guatemalan military that were signed in 1996. Today the URNG functions as a legitimate political party in Guatemala.

---

[9] *Partido Guatemalteco del Trabajo* [10] *Unidad Revolucionaria Nacional de Guatemala*

El Salvador

El Salvador's progressive Left did not immediately adopt guerrilla warfare in the 1960s. The influence of the communist party (PCS)[11] was much more significant in El Salvador than elsewhere in the region, and it had close ties to the Soviet Union, which opposed the Cuban model. By the 1970s several factions within the Salvadoran Communist Party had left the party to pursue a guerrilla strategy. And by 1975, the Communist Party had also committed itself to armed struggle. In 1980 five distinct revolutionary groups united to form the Farabundo Martí National Liberation Front (FMLN).[12] The FMLN launched two major offensives in the 1980s but ultimately was unable to achieve a military victory. After the end of the Cold War, both the Salvadoran army and the FMLN were motivated to negotiate a peace. Like the URNG, the FMLN continues to be a political party today in El Salvador.

Nicaragua

The Sandinista National Liberation Front (FSLN),[13] like most of the armed revolutionary movements in the Caribbean, was born in response to the success of the Cuban Revolution. Nicaragua was ruled by a repressive and corrupt dynastic dictatorship in 1959, and the various armed opposition groups in the country came together fairly early to form a unified national opposition front. The United States historically also had a much heavier hand in Nicaragua (occupying the country militarily for more than two decades at the beginning of the twentieth century) which led to widespread and strong anti-US sentiment in the country.

The FSLN is the only armed movement discussed in this book (besides that in Cuba) that actually came to power. Its armed movement was able to coordinate a widespread popular insurrection across the country that resulted in a military victory. It was in power for just over a decade (1979–1989) and stepped down when it lost a popular election in 1989 to a coalition of parties that opposed the Revolution. Despite this, it emerged from this electoral defeat as the largest political party in the country, and it has since regained the presidency in regular elections.

---

[11] *Partido Comunista de El Salvador*
[12] *Frente Farabundo Martí para la Liberación Nacional*
[13] *Frente Sandinista de Liberación Nacional*

Colombia

Colombia's armed revolutionary movements emerged in a distinct context from its Central American neighbors. For most of Colombia's modern history, the country has been rife with civil and political conflict. An extremely violent conflict (called *La Violencia*) between the two major political parties took almost half a million lives during the 1950s; several campesino-based self-defense groups emerged mostly with the intention of maintaining their autonomy from the state and keeping national military forces out of their communities. By the 1960s and in response to the Cuban Revolution, many of these rural-based guerrillas began to reformulate their struggle in alliance with other social actors who had a more explicitly socialist or Marxist orientation. The National Liberation Army (ELN)[14] and the Rebel Armed Forces of Colombia (FARC)[15] were both born in the mid-1960s and the 19th of April Movement (M-19) was founded in 1973 from the remnants of the Leftist-inspired civil political movement (ANAPO),[16] which had been shut out of the so-called democratic political process.

The M-19 was able to successfully negotiate a peace accord with the Colombian state in 1990, but for various reasons this peace proved elusive to the other guerrilla groups in this country. After the Colombian Congress ratified a peace accord between the government and the FARC in December 2016, the most significant actors in this long-lived conflict laid down their arms. An agreement between the government and the ELN will hopefully mark a definitive end to this violent period of Colombia's history.

Puerto Rico

Puerto Rico's case is unique in that the movements for Puerto Rican independence predated the Cold War, and the independence of which they spoke was literal rather than metaphorical. Puerto Rico's status *vis-à-vis* the United States is unique. Puerto Ricans are US citizens, and they are entitled to many of the benefits of citizenship. Nevertheless they are not part of the United States proper, and they have no representation in Congress. Their relationship with the United States is explicitly and legally neocolonial dependency.

While the independence movement in Puerto Rico has its origins in the early twentieth century, the "new struggle for independence" corresponds

---

[14] *Ejército de Liberación Nacional*   [15] *Fuerzas Armadas Revolucionarias de Colombia*
[16] *Alianza Nacional Popular*

with the Cold War time frame of this volume and is the subject here. The chapter on Puerto Rico tells the story of the four most important revolutionary armed movements from the period: the Pro-Independence Movement (MPI),[17] the Puerto Rican Socialist Party (PSP),[18] the Armed Commanders for Liberation (CAL),[19] and the Revolutionary Workers Party-Puerto Rican Boricua Popular Army (PRTP-EPB)[20] or the "Macheteros." All of these movements evolved in response to the success of the Cuban Revolution. But they also operated inside of the United States, as well as on the island. Therefore they were also impacted by the anti-Vietnam protest movement and the civil rights movement inside the United States.

BROAD CONSIDERATIONS

Enormous diversity existed among the dozens of Cold War–era armed groups in the Caribbean Basin. The horrific nature of the violence directed at these groups and the civilian populations in the most-affected countries often overshadows the real political identities and agency of the revolutionary militants of this era.

By the middle of the 1970s, the protection of basic human rights and consideration for the physical security of the civilian population began to take precedence over other political and social issues that had motivated many to take up arms in the first place. As the illegitimacy and illegality of the counterinsurgency campaigns became obvious, the desire for real liberal democracy also began to overshadow the more dogmatic and militant Leftist ideologies of the Cold War.

In this defensive context the human rights movement emerged in Latin America. While initially connected to the larger popular struggle, the human rights movement made pragmatic use of international legal instruments to oppose the state, and to protect themselves and the organizations with which they had established networks of solidarity. The appeal to the United Nations, the international community, and international law forced an ideological shift toward liberalism.

By the time many of the opposing military regimes were deposed or peace treaties had been negotiated, there was a need to emphasize human rights and the crimes of the state. This made it politically necessary to diminish the emphasis on the more radical political objectives of the

---

[17] *Movimiento Pro-Independencia*   [18] *Partido Socialista Puertorriqueño*
[19] *Comandos Armados de Liberación*
[20] *Partido Revolucionario de los Trabajadores Puertorriqueños-Ejército Popular Boricua*

armed movements, as well as the real political identities of the protagonists who were committed to armed revolutionary struggle. The human
rights community emphasized the illegality of state-sponsored terrorism.
In an attempt to reject the thesis of *dos demonios*, or "two demons,"
popular movements, and particularly the human rights movement,
emphasized the innocence of the victims.[21] In emphasizing the illegal
and extrajudicial nature of the violence that was meted out by the state,
the political identities of those who actively and in many cases violently
opposed these regimes were often obscured. This volume seeks to redis-
cover the complex and diverse character of revolutionary politics during
this era.

TRANSITIONS TO DEMOCRACY

The stories of armed revolutionary movements in the Caribbean Basin do
not all end with the fall of the Berlin Wall in 1989. These manifestations of
popular revolutionary struggles mostly transitioned into civil society and
liberal political democracy in the decades since the wars ended. Many of
these organizations function as legitimate and popular political parties in
the region today. This volume also considers the transitions these groups
made from military organizations to political parties. The final chapter of
the book will look at the contemporary political realities of all five
countries. To understand New Social Movements and the new progressive
politics of the region, we have to consider the revolutionary politics of
their predecessors.

Suggested Reading

Brands, Hal. *Latin America's Cold War*. Cambridge, MA: Harvard University
   Press, 2010.
Chomsky, Aviva. *A History of the Cuban Revolution*. New York: Wiley-
   Blackwell, 2010.

---

[21] The theory of the two demons was promulgated in Argentina during the transition to
democracy. *Dos demonios* emphasized that the nation had suffered from a conflict
between two warring factions (the guerrilla insurgency and the military). This idea was
a way of placing partial responsibility for the abuses perpetrated by the state on armed
revolutionary movements. The idea was transplanted to the Caribbean Basin as well, as
a way of making transitional justice more palatable to elites or others who supported
military rule. In reality, the vast majority of deaths and incidences of war crimes during
these conflicts were verifiably attributed to the regular military forces and paramilitary
groups (death squads) that supported them.

DeFronzo, James. *Revolutions and Revolutionary Movements*, 5th ed. Boulder, CO: Westview Press, 2015.

De La Pedraja, Rene. *Wars of Latin America, 1948–1982*. Jefferson, NC: McFarland and Company, Inc., 2013.

Grandin, Greg. *The Last Colonial Massacre: Latin America in the Cold War*. Chicago: University of Chicago Press, 2004.

Grandin, Greg and Gilbert Joseph, Eds. *A Century of Revolution: Insurgent and Counterinsurgent Violence during Latin America's Long Cold War*. Durham, NC: Duke University Press, 2010.

Guevara, Ernesto "Che". *Guerrilla Warfare*. New York: Ocean Press, 2006.

Perez-Stable, Marifeli. *The Cuban Revolution: Origins, Course and Legacy*, 3rd ed. New York: Oxford University Press, 2011.

Selbin, Eric. *Modern Latin American Revolutions*, 2nd ed. Boulder, CO: Westview Press, 1999.

Stout, Nancy. *One Day in December: Celia Sánchez and the Cuban Revolution*. New York: Monthly Review Press, 2013.

Wickham-Crowley, Timothy. *Guerrillas and Revolution in Latin America: A Comparative Study of Insurgents and Regimes since 1956*. Princeton: Princeton University Press, 1992.

Reading on Marxist Theory in Latin America

Debray, Regís. *Revolution in the Revolution?* New York: Grove Press, 1968.

Harnecker, Marta. *Fidel Castro's Political Strategy: From Moncada to Victory*. New York: Pathfinder, 1989.

Harnecker, Marta. *Revolución social: Lenin y América Latina*. Mexico: Siglo XXI, 1986.

Harnecker, Marta. *A World to Build: New Paths toward Twenty-first Century Socialism*. New York: Monthly Review Press, 2015.

Mariátegui, José Carlos. *José Carlos Mariátegui: An Anthology* (Harry J. Vanden and Marc Becker, Eds.). New York: Monthly Review Press, 2011.

Torres, Camilo. *Revolutionary Priest, The Complete Writings and Messages of Camilo Torres* (John Gerassi, Ed.). New York: Random House, 1971.

Films

Burn! (1968)
Che: A Revolutionary Life (2008)
Cuba: Defending Socialism, Resisting Imperialism (2010)
Memorias del Subdesarollo (1968 Cuba)
PBS The American Experience: Fidel Castro (2004)

2

Armed Revolutionary Struggle in Guatemala

Guatemala was the first country in the region to experience an armed revolutionary movement launched directly in response to the victory of the 26th of July Movement in Cuba. Guatemala and Cuba were similar in that they both had extreme rural poverty, and high levels of inequality between rural and urban areas. As had been the case with Cuba, Guatemalan campesinos had been displaced by the rapid growth of an agro-export economy. A large percentage of the population lived in an isolated mountainous part of the country, while migrating to commercial plantations for seasonal employment. It was certainly true that Guatemala met Che Guevara's "objective" criterion for a successful revolutionary movement. Guatemala was the poorest country in Central America, and one of the poorest countries in the hemisphere. Guevara emphasized the idea that abject poverty would motivate potential militant revolutionaries, and that the conditions of rural poverty in countries where campesinos were largely ignored by the state would provide the perfect conditions for guerrilla warfare. Guatemala seemed in many ways to be the obvious place for the next guerrilla foco.

Despite the economic similarities between the two countries, there were also key differences between Cuba and Guatemala. While Cuba endured the scourge of African slavery during the Spanish colonization, Guatemala's indigenous population was subjected to a different kind of racial and ethnic oppression. The majority of Guatemala's population is racially and ethnically indigenous. The Maya peoples of Guatemala were also enslaved, but they were *not* subjected to a system of chattel slavery, whereby they were sold as "property." They were conquered by a Spanish military invasion of their homeland. The conquest of the Maya territories in Central America resulted in the death of about 90 percent of the population. It was a genocidal conquest. The Maya were forcibly converted to Christianity and then colonized by a feudal empire. They survived the conquest and colonization of their lands by maintaining their distance (when possible) from the Spanish colonizers. They retreated into more remote and less hospitable lands at higher elevations. Although they were also exploited for their labor, they coexisted with the Spanish in a more feudal (and less capitalist) land-labor arrangement for several centuries. This resulted in Guatemala's unique modern ethnic makeup. A small majority of the population remains as ethnically Mayan. This (indigenous) majority is made up of 23 distinct linguistic groups with unique ethnic characteristics. A very substantial minority is also racially indigenous or *mestizo*,[1] but they do not *ethnically* identify as indigenous. These people are referred to as *ladino* in the Guatemalan context. The designation of "ladino" implies someone of low economic status who is not identifiably indigenous. It is a strictly ethnic term that refers to language (Spanish) and culture (Hispanic or non-indigenous). Then there is a small minority of the population who identify as "white" or "European."

In the mid-twentieth century, Guatemala was a racially and ethnically divided nation. It suffered from virulent racism that extended from elites down into the campesino classes. Armed revolutionary movements in the country had to grapple with this racism – often euphemistically referred to as the "Indian question" – and the early leaders of the guerrilla movements (who were mostly non-Maya) were not immune from the historical wound of racism.

In the end, the civil war that developed in Guatemala was among the most devastating in the region. The counterinsurgency strategy that had emerged by the early 1980s was called "genocide" by the UN-brokered Commission for Historical Clarification (CEH). Tens of thousands of civilians died in the conflict, most of whom (more than 90 percent) died at the hands of the Guatemalan military. The vast majority of the victims were Maya. More than 1 million people were forcibly displaced during the worst years of the war. There were at least 626 documented massacres (where entire villages were destroyed), and many other Maya communities were occupied by the Guatemalan military, and in some cases turned into concentration camps, euphemistically called "model villages."[2]

---

[1] A *mestizo* is someone who is of mixed European and indigenous ancestry. It is a racial term.

[2] Commission for Historical Clarification (CEH), *Guatemala: Memory of Silence*. Available in pdf at www.aaas.org/sites/default/files/migrate/uploads/mos_en.pdf.

The armed conflict in Guatemala was costly by any measure. The issues that motivated the armed revolutionaries were complex and difficult. Guatemala remains an extremely poor country with high levels of inequality and systemic violence. More than 20 years have passed since the peace accords officially ended the armed conflict. A marked remilitarization has occurred in recent years. As a result of the rise of criminal violence in the country, overall levels of violence have not significantly declined since the end of the conflict. There have been improvements in levels of political freedom and representation, but it is important to reexamine the history of the brutal conflict that gave birth to the new "democratic" nation. This chapter will explore the history of armed revolutionary struggle in Guatemala during the 1960s, 1970s, and 1980s up until the peace accords in the 1990s. This history is explored in three phases: 1960–1972, 1972–1985, and concluding with a transition to electoral politics (1985–1996). The analysis will elucidate the ideological and structural evolution of the movements, as well as their transition to civil society after the abandonment of armed struggle. The Cold War came to Guatemala well before the military victory of the Cuban 26th of July Movement in 1959. When the reformist government of Jacobo Arbenz was overthrown in a coup orchestrated by the US government in June 1954, the Cold War had already begun to exact a heavy toll on the people of Guatemala.

GUATEMALA'S COLD WAR CONTEXT

Guatemala's Revolution (1944–1954) ended when the US Central Intelligence Agency (CIA) orchestrated a small invasion of Guatemalan nationals from the Honduran border. The invasion (called "Operation Success" by the CIA) was more of a psychological victory than a military one. Believing that the invading force was more substantial than it was, and unable to rouse the Guatemalan army from its barracks to defend the reformist government, President Jacobo Arbenz left the country on June 27, 1954. It was a humiliating (if almost bloodless) defeat for Guatemalan popular self-determination. The US interests in Guatemala were certainly tied to the United Fruit Company, which had direct connections to the Eisenhower White House as well as the CIA. But the soul of US opposition to the Guatemalan "Revolution" and Arbenz's agrarian reform program was rooted in a paranoid anti-communism. It was the height of the McCarthy era in the United States; although Arbenz himself was no communist, the Communist Party (the PGT)[3] was present within the Arbenz administration, the labor movement, and the agrarian committees that were set up to carry out the Agrarian Reform Act (Decree 900, 1952). The coup in Guatemala and the purge of communists there were motivated by fear of communism, and a belief that the United States was free to assert its prerogative in Guatemala with virtually no consideration for Guatemalan sovereignty or national interests.[4]

The period between 1954 and 1960 was a tumultuous one of transition for the Guatemalan state and its armed forces. Carlos Castillo Armas, who had led the skeletal invasion in 1954, was the president until he was assassinated in 1957. He was perceived as a puppet of the United States, and the dismantling of the reforms of the Revolution, the demobilization of workers and peasants, and the purging of communists (and other would-be sympathizers) were in large part directed by US officials. These often-violent policies resulted in increasing nationalism and anti-US sentiment, even among the armed forces. General Miguel Ydígoras Fuentes, the perennial presidential hopeful, returned from his post as ambassador to Colombia to run again for president. After a fraudulent election (in which his opponent – Miguel Ortiz Passarelli – was declared the winner), a failed coup attempt by Ydígoras and his followers, and a new election, Ydígoras assumed the presidency early in 1958. During the entire period of Ydígoras's rule, public demonstrations, mass mobilizations, and vocal opposition to the regime were common. Most of the opposition came from urban sectors (students, urban workers, former trade unionists, etc.), but it was not limited to the capital. These public protests were often fraught with violence and pitted the armed forces against those who protested fraud and corruption.

ARMED REVOLUTIONARY STRUGGLE IN THE FIRST PHASE (1960–1972)

On November 13, 1960, approximately 400 Guatemalan military officers staged a coup on the Ydígoras government. The officers were opposed to the internal corruption of both the military and the government. Opposition was widespread among the officers to the training of Cuban exiles (by US forces) on Guatemalan soil in preparation for the Bay of Pigs

---

[3] *Partido Guatemalteco del Trabajo*

[4] Stephen Schlesinger and Stephen Kinzer, *Bitter Fruit: The Story of the American Coup in Guatemala* (Cambridge, MA: Harvard University Press, 1999).

invasion. And a core of officers still sympathized with the nationalist goals of the Guatemalan Revolution.[5] Although the coup attempt failed, several of the leaders, including Marco Antonio Yon Sosa and Luís Turcios Lima, escaped to the banana-growing region of Izábal; by the spring of 1961, they occupied that region in the name of their newly formed guerrilla organization, the Alejandro de León Rebel Movement of November 13 (MR-13).[6] They initiated their guerrilla operations by attacking two army posts and robbing a United Fruit Company office in the early months of 1961.[7]

In the meantime the Communist Party of Guatemala (PGT) had been outlawed after the fall of Arbenz in the summer of 1954. It continued to function as a clandestine organization with the goal of reorganizing the popular sectors as well as the "progressive bourgeoisie." The PGT held a Congress in 1960 at which it agreed to the use of "all means of struggle" (implying the growing acceptability of violence). The Central Committee decided to initiate an armed struggle in 1961. In March 1962, it organized a guerrilla army in Concua, Baja Verapaz, called the October 20th Front, in honor of the (1944) Guatemalan Revolution. The Guatemalan army almost immediately decimated this guerrilla army.[8]

One of the original leaders of the military coup against Ydígoras, and one of the co-founders of the MR-13, Luís Turcios Lima, approached various urban-based political parties – including moderate "bourgeois" organizations – throughout 1961 in an attempt to forge political alliances without much success. After its failed attempt at armed insurrection in March 1962, the PGT publicly pledged a willingness to ally with the MR-13.[9] In December 1962, the MR-13 decided to ally itself with the PGT's failed 20th of October Front and also a group of students from the University of San Carlos who had organized mass demonstrations against the Ydígoras government in March and April 1962. The MR-13, the

---

[5] Jacobo Arbenz was himself a colonel in the Guatemalan army, and there was a small base of support for the democratic ideals of the Revolution within the military until the reconsolidation of the armed forces after the coup of 1963.

[6] *Movimiento Rebelde 13 de Noviembre*. Alejandro de León was one of the original leaders of the 1960 attempted coup. He was among the officers who returned from exile in March 1961 to pursue the struggle against the Ydígoras regime. De León was captured and assassinated soon after his return to Guatemala.

[7] Gabriel Aguilera Peralta and Jorge Romero Imery et al., *Dialéctica del terror en Guatemala* (San José, Costa Rica: EDUCA, 1981), 106.

[8] Aguilera Peralta and Romero Imery, Dialéctica del terror en Guatemala, 107–108.

[9] Richard Gott, *Guerrilla Movements in Latin America* (Garden City, NY: Doubleday, 1971), 50; Aguilera Peralta and Romero Imery, *Dialéctica del terror en Guatemala*, 107–108.

PGT's 20th of October Front, and the students (who called themselves the April 12th Movement) came together to form the Rebel Armed Forces, or the FAR.[10]

Internal Structure during the First Phase (1960–1972)

The FAR was officially responsible for handling the military strategy of the PGT. Despite this, the power of both political decision making and military strategy in reality migrated toward the leadership of the Communist PGT. The PGT remained at the top of the vertical hierarchy. The leadership of the PGT organized a political directorate within the FAR called the United Resistance Front, or FUR.[11] While the FUR did not control the guerrillas, it did control the mobilization strategy for new guerrilla recruits and so was able to exert considerable influence. The Communist Party (through the FUR) dictated ideology, and military decisions (justified by ideological necessity) were also made by the Communist directorate. Yon Sosa's MR-13 had no representation within the FUR, and leaders of the MR-13 felt pressured into a situation in which they were being guided primarily by outside political leadership.[12]

In March 1965, Luís Turcios Lima tried to unify the three factions of the FAR (MR-13, the PGT, and his own Edgar Ibarra Guerrilla Front [FGEI][13], which was already officially part of the MR-13) by calling a meeting of the leaders of all the groups. When Marco Antonio Yon Sosa refused to attend, Turcios separated his FGEI from the MR-13. Consequently, the MR-13, led by Yon Sosa, declared that it was splitting from the FAR in its "Declaration of Sierra de las Minas." The split was fundamentally the result of the ideological differences between what had become a Trotskyist-oriented MR-13[14] and the more conservative Communists of the PGT.[15] Although Turcios and another FAR leader, Luís Trejo Esquivel, had already begun to distance themselves and the FAR from both the MR-13 and the PGT in a position paper they issued in October 1964, it appears that a renewed alliance with the PGT was

---

[10] *Fuerzas Armadas Rebeldes*   [11] *Frente Unido de Resistencia*

[12] Adolfo Gilly, "Part Two: The Guerrilla Movement in Guatemala," *Monthly Review* (June 1965): 7–41; Gott, Guerrilla Movements in Latin America, 62.

[13] *Frente Guerrillera Edgar Ibarra*

[14] Yon-Sosa considered himself to be Trotskyist during this time. He believed that a successful revolution had to be class based and he urged the rejection of nationalism within the movement.

[15] Gott, Guerrilla Movements in Latin America, 62; Gilly, "Part Two," 16.

nevertheless inevitable.[16] Despite latent ideological differences between Turcios and his FGEI and the PGT, in response to the rupture between Yon Sosa and Turcios, the PGT agreed to more fully support the armed struggle of the FAR (and thus the FGEI). The FGEI expanded its base and grew significantly between 1965 and 1966. In 1966, Turcios decided to strengthen the political base of the struggle by going to Guatemala City and personally joining the PGT. He was then killed in a car accident on October 2, 1966. This was a blow to morale, and his leadership was not easy to replace.

Two years later in 1968, the FGEI and the FAR broke away from the PGT and allied themselves once again with MR-13. Later that year, the head of the FGEI, Camilo Sanchez (who replaced Turcios after his death in 1966), was captured and killed. Yon Sosa (and his MR-13) again withdrew from the FAR. Divisions that were both ideological and personalistic continued to plague the FAR, but by 1970 the FAR had been effectively neutralized by the counterinsurgency strategy of the army.

The changing alliances of these guerrilla organizations were extremely complicated – and these shifts affected the vertical structures (the

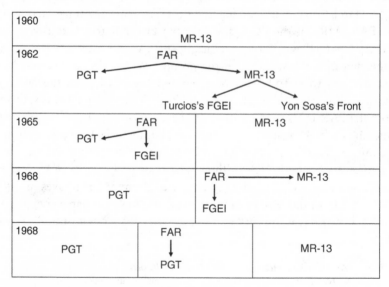

FIGURE 2.1 Organizational chart of the historical evolution of guerrilla organizations during Phase 1

[16] Timothy Wickham-Crowley, *Guerrillas and Revolution in Latin America* (Princeton, NJ: Princeton University Press, 1992), 39.

hierarchies) of every guerrilla group. Moreover, the ideological differences and changes had a direct impact upon the horizontal organizational structures as well. For example, Trotskyists (mostly in the MR-13) favored the organization of local noncombatant peasant committees, while the Guevara-ists and the PGT did not. Consequently, internal structures – both vertical and horizontal – were constantly shifting during this period, on both the national and local levels (see Figure 2.1).

Mobilization Strategy during the First Phase (1960–1972)

When the MR-13 first began its operations, no campesinos were recruited into the rank and file; the MR-13 was entirely composed of disaffected military men, most of whom were second-tier officers.[17] After the creation of the FAR, Yon Sosa's front of the MR-13 cultivated a broad campesino base among the ladino population in the lowlands, establishing campesino committees in many towns and challenging the legitimacy of the standing governments in those municipalities. In late 1966, the MR-13 claimed to have more than 500 families organized into campesino committees. Although the towns had local "defense patrols" that were supposed to repel the Guatemalan army, they were ineffectual in this task. Eventually this approach toward guerrilla warfare (which was rooted in an ideological commitment to Che Guevara's foquismo) proved to be the downfall of the MR-13, as these campesino committees were perfect targets for the military given their lack of military training and their stationary status. They were in effect noncombatants who were "set up" for reprisal by the armed forces. Because this mobilization strategy proved to have disastrous consequences for both the campesinos who were recruited and the MR-13 organization, the self-labeled Trotskyists who had urged this strategy were eventually discredited within the movement.

The Edgar Ibarra Guerrilla Front (FGEI), headed by Turcios Lima, enjoyed more military success than Yon Sosa's Eastern Front of the MR-13. The FGEI was based in the Sierra de las Minas in Zacapa and was composed of a wider base of popular combatants – members of the communist youth organization, students, workers, and (mostly ladino) campesinos. Turcios was critical of the Trotskyist tactics of Yon Sosa's front of the MR-13, and he was also critical of the PGT's more Soviet-line conciliatory stance with the political bourgeoisie.

---

[17] Gott, *Guerrilla Movements in Latin America*, 45–53; Aguilera Peralta and Romero Imery, *Dialéctica del terror en Guatemala*, 106–107.

The PGT was composed of urban-based intellectuals and their mobilization strategy was almost entirely urban based. This urban strategy, as well as the ladino-focused strategy of the other organizations was problematic in a country that was overwhelmingly rural and ethnically Mayan.

Ideology during the First Phase (1960–1972)

The MR-13's strategy in this early period was to attack military installations; it was not planning a "prolonged people's war," but rather a quick overthrow of the Ydígoras regime. The rebels in these early months were primarily nationalists in the model of Augusto Sandino in Nicaragua.

Although its members came directly out of the PGT, the October 20th guerrilla front also claimed to have modest nationalist intentions as well as seeking to overthrow the Ydígoras regime. They claimed to have modeled themselves after the broad-based coalition of nationalist "revolutionaries" who overthrew the dictatorship of Jorge Ubíco in the fall of 1944.

As time went by, the differences between the ideologies and tactics of the MR-13 and the FUR (which represented the views of the urban leadership of the Communist Party) widened. The guerrilla experience radicalized the MR-13 fighters, while the PGT took a more conciliatory stance, which was deeply rooted in the experiences of the Russian and Chinese Revolutions. The FUR was increasingly withdrawing from its commitment to a radical overthrow of the Guatemalan government; instead, it hoped to use the guerrillas as a bargaining chip that would eventually allow it to participate in electoral politics as it had between 1944 and 1954.

The MR-13, influenced by the abject conditions of poverty in the countryside, saw its own relationship to the masses differently from the Communist leadership in both the FUR and the PGT. Agrarian reform became its most critical concern. The leadership of the MR-13 was increasingly drawn toward Marxism and eventually toward Trotskyism, which caused significant division within the MR-13 itself. The second front, based in the eastern part of the country and led by Luís Trejo, completely dispersed after a struggle broke out between communists and anti-communists within their ranks.[18] The Trotskyites urged the rebels to attempt a more sweeping mass insurrection. That is, they wanted to incorporate campesinos and workers into one large revolutionary

---

[18] Gott, *Guerrilla Movements in Latin America*, 64.

insurrectionist movement. Francisco Amado Granados, a member of the international directorate of the MR-13 said in 1965:

We plan to organize underground committees of armed workers and also students similar to those now existing among peasants; and we shall promote trade unionism, legal or underground; and we shall prepare the conditions and mentalities of the masses for a revolutionary workers' *central*. And our slogan, which is already spreading, will become a reality for important sectors of the population; "workers, peasants, students, arm yourselves."[19]

The FGEI wing of the MR-13 followed a more Guevara-ist line, emphasizing the rural foco to the exclusion of anything else. It also opposed the less confrontational stance of the PGT. These ideological and tactical divisions eventually resulted in the FAR (which came to represent the FGEI), the MR-13, and the PGT splitting apart and operating independently of one another. These divisions made all social movements in Guatemala more vulnerable to state-sponsored terror.

The original motivations for armed struggle in Guatemala did not emanate from the poor or the indigenous people. They were nationalistic and formed in opposition to blatant US interference and disregard for Guatemalan sovereignty and interests. The context of the Cold War altered the ideologies of the armed movements and added both complexity and a kind of dogmatism that never seemed entirely appropriate to the national economic and ethnic context of Guatemala. The poorest and most vulnerable Guatemalans suffered because of the dogmatism and the somewhat foolhardy approach to guerrilla warfare these early revolutionaries adopted. The Guatemalan military, with US backing, also showed itself to be capable of extreme brutality which was justified by the "threat" of communism. The political system in Cold War Guatemala lost all semblance of democratic rule.

ARMED REVOLUTIONARY STRUGGLE IN THE SECOND PHASE (1972–1985)

The changing economic roles of indigenous people from the highlands of Guatemala brought Maya people into increasing contact with non-Maya. By migrating to southern coastal plantations and to urban areas, indigenous campesinos learned Spanish and became intertwined in the national economy. The violence that was at least in part both the cause and

[19] Gilly, "Part Two," 29; Gott, *Guerrilla Movements in Latin America*, 65.

consequence of armed revolutionary struggle also had drastic repercussions for the indigenous populations. The Ecumenical Program for Inter-American Communication and Action (EPICA) estimates that more than 48 percent of all indigenous residents of the highlands (1,225,600 people in total) were murdered, "disappeared," or had fled the region by 1983.[20] Many factors (e.g., racism and targeted violence by the state, changes within the Catholic Church, the cooperative movement and its "consciousness raising" efforts) combined to bring indigenous people more fully into the civil conflict that was marked by a brutal scorched earth counterinsurgency campaign that resulted in the murder of tens of thousands of noncombatants.

The genocidal tactics of the counterinsurgency campaign of the Guatemalan military dictatorship had important implications for the way both revolutionary combatants and popular noncombatants organized. The rural civilian population was increasingly compelled to take defensive actions to survive. The relationships between the armed groups and the non-militant "popular movement" were strengthened in many parts of the country because of the indiscriminate violence of the Guatemalan military.

Internal Structure during the Second Phase (1972–1985)

Between 1968 and 1972, guerrilla leaders began to reevaluate their failure to take power during the first phase. The failure of the FAR in the 1960s was not attributed to poor military strategy so much as it was deemed a political failure. The FAR leadership correctly conceded that campesino masses were never fully integrated into the struggle. The repression, in effect, only further isolated the guerrillas from the popular sectors (*la base*).[21] In addition to the personalistic divisions that split the leadership and the rank and file of the organizations, the guerrillas blamed the leadership of the PGT for their failures. The guerrilla commanders believed that they had wrongly deferred to the PGT with regard to several key strategic decisions. This, they believed, resulted in a misguided political orientation of the struggle, most importantly the unfortunate decision *not* to organize in the predominantly indigenous

---

[20] Luisa Frank and Philip Wheaton, *Indian Guatemala: Path to Liberation* (Washington, DC: EPICA Task Force, 1984), 92.

[21] Suzanne Jonas, *Battle for Guatemala* (Boulder: Westview, 1991) 135–136; "Los Fundamentos Teóricos de las Fuerzas Armadas rebeldes," document produced by FAR Dirección Nacional Ejecutiva, Guatemala, March 1973. CITGUA archives (Mexico City).

central and western highlands. The PGT had viewed the Maya paternalistically through a decidedly racist lens. The Communist Party firmly believed that because of their "backwardness," they lacked revolutionary potential. During the second phase, the FAR remained autonomous of the PGT.

The remnants of Turcios Lima's FGEI in 1972 reentered Guatemala from Mexico (where they had been in exile since 1969) and began to reorganize in the predominantly indigenous Ixcán region of El Quiché. This new guerrilla front became the Guerrilla Army of the Poor (EGP).[22] They eventually organized three new military fronts in the highlands: the "Ho Chi Minh Front" (centered in El Quiché), the "Ernesto Che Guevara Front" (centered in Huehuetenango), and the "Augusto César Sandino Front" (also in El Quiché).[23]

Another splinter group of the FAR, which had also been critical of the racist and paternalistic tendencies of the guerrilla movement of the 1960s, began operating clandestinely in 1971 in the area around Lake Atitlan and on the southern coastal plain. This organization called itself the FAR/Western Regional[24] in the early 1970s. Eventually this group renamed itself the Revolutionary Organization of the People in Arms (ORPA)[25] and in 1979 emerged publicly.

The PGT barely survived organizationally during the 1970s. The two most successful guerrilla groups rejected its leadership role, and it continued to suffer from the same personalistic and dogmatic ideological divisions that had defined it in the 1960s. It did continue "the struggle" within small segments of the urban labor force, and among proletarianized workers on the southern coast but did not have any significant military success.[26]

The FAR, EGP, ORPA, and PGT united into a national broad front organization – the Guatemalan National Revolutionary Unity (URNG)[27] in January 1982. The creation of a united umbrella organization did not imply ideological homogeneity of the member organizations, or even a common bureaucratic or political infrastructure, but it did represent a new degree of flexibility and cooperation. The ability of these organizations to put aside rigid ideological differences stands in contrast to the

---

[22] *Ejercito Guerillero de los Pobres*

[23] Concerned Guatemala Scholars, *Dare to Struggle, Dare to Win* (Brooklyn: Concerned Guatemala Scholars, 1982), 19–21; Longman Group Limited, *Latin American Political Movements* (London: Longman, 1985), 145.

[24] *FAR/Regional del Occidente*   [25] *Organización Revolucionaria del Pueblo en Armas*

[26] Jonas, *Battle*, 138.   [27] *Unidad Revolucionaria Nacional de Guatemala*

original FAR, which was supposed to represent the alliance between the M-13 and the PGT.

The organization of the URNG ran parallel to a similar kind of unity within the popular movement as a whole in Guatemala. By the mid-1980s, much of the country was at least informally organized in opposition to the brutal and illegitimate military dictatorship. This forced the military to cede power to an elected civilian government in 1985. While this new civilian government was not able to subordinate the military, it did mark the beginning of the end of the civil war.

Mobilization Strategy during the Second Phase (1972–1985)

The FAR organized among elements of urban labor, and campesinos in the southern coastal plain plantations, and in the Petén. In contrast to the mobilization strategy of the 1960s, during the second phase the FAR concentrated on education of the popular sectors and giving the rank and file a personal stake in the struggle.[28]

Like the new FAR, the EGP rejected the Communist Party's evaluation and analysis of the revolutionary potential of the indigenous population. The EGP mobilized the campesino base that had been politically influenced by changing labor relations (toward a larger itinerant migrant rural workforce in the service of agro-export), liberation theology and the changing Catholic Church, and education. Many of these new recruits of the EGP were ethnically self-identified Maya.[29]

The ORPA was also committed to the political organization of indigenous campesinos. More than 90 percent of the membership of ORPA was indigenous, as well as some of the local leadership. Nevertheless, its national leadership was still overwhelmingly ladino.[30] Despite the increased sensitivity to the reality of racism by the guerrilla leadership, guerrilla leaders were unable to divest themselves entirely of the

---

[28] Jonas, *Battle*, 137.

[29] Chapters 3 and 5 contain more extensive discussions of liberation theology. For a discussion of the changing nature of the *campesinado*, see Ricardo Falla, *Quiché rebelde* (Guatemala: USAC, 1978); José Luís Chea, *Guatemala: La cruz fragmentada* (Costa Rica: FLACSO, 1988); José Manuel Fernández, *El Comité de Unidad Campesina*, Cuaderno 2 (Guatemala: CERCA, 1988); Carlos Figueroa Ibarra, *El Proletariado rural en el agro guatemalteco* (Guatemala: USAC, 1980); and Luisa Frank and Philip Wheaton, *Indian Guatemala: Path to Liberation*).

[30] Wickham-Crowley, *Guerrillas*, 217–218.

paternalistic attitudes that were so deeply imbedded in the history of the country.

The PGT was a skeletal organization during the 1970s and 1980s. It continued to try to mobilize urban trade unionists, student groups, and to a lesser degree within agricultural trade unions on the southern coast.[31] This mobilization strategy of working within organized labor and urban middle-class elements proved to be weak as the PGT attracted a very small following during this period.[32]

Ideology during the Second Phase (1972–1985)

The FAR continued its commitment to armed struggle during the second phase, but its guerrilla base was comparatively small and concentrated in the Petén. Like the PGT, the FAR also worked within urban trade unions in Guatemala City and the more urban department of Chimaltenango. Its ideological tendencies were less dogmatic during the second phase. The FAR spent a considerable amount of time during this period engaged in educating (or propagandizing) the masses.[33]

The EGP was influenced in the 1970s and 1980s by the examples of prolonged struggle in China and Vietnam. Consequently, it launched its own version of a "prolonged people's war." The EGP worked for three years developing a popular base among the campesino masses before committing its first public act in 1975 – the assassination of Luís Arenas Barrera. Arenas was a large landholder in the Ixcán area who was known as the "Tiger" or the "Jaguar" of Ixcán because of his brutality and cruelty toward campesinos.[34]

The ideological leadership of the EGP thoughtfully considered the "Indian question" throughout the 1970s to develop a sophisticated understanding of the multiethnic Guatemala toward which it was striving. Its revolutionary vision sought to truly integrate the indigenous concerns about ethnic oppression with the more general concerns of economic exploitation (or class struggle). The EGP, while clearly still influenced by

---

[31] Tom Barry and Deb Preusch, *The Central American Fact Book* (New York: Grove Press, 1986), 233.

[32] Wickham-Crowley, *Guerrillas*, 217; Jonas, *Battle*, 138.

[33] Wickham-Crowley, *Guerrillas*, 224; Jonas, *Battle*, 136–137; Barry and Preusch, *The Central American Fact Book*, 232–233.

[34] Jonas, *Battle*, 137. Mario Payeras, *Days of the Jungle: The Testimony of a Guatemalan Guerillero* (New York: Monthly Review Press, 1983), 71–77.

Marxism, was also profoundly influenced by the indigenous perspective of its members during the 1970s.[35]

The ORPA began carefully and clandestinely developing its base of support in 1971 and committed its first public act of violence in September 1979. The ORPA, like the EGP, was influenced by Marxism, but it was even more influenced by its indigenous base. It officially stood for "an end to racism" and "the development of indigenous culture."[36] Further emphasizing its autonomy, it officially rejected association with the Soviet Union. Geographically, it complemented the EGP, operating in the central western highlands, and among the indigenous populations in the departments of San Marcos, Totonicapán, Quetzaltenango, and Sololá (in the area surrounding Lake Atitlan).[37]

The PGT maintained its conservative posture and its links to Soviet-line communism for most of the second phase. The organization rejected armed struggle until 1978 when part of the leadership nucleus of the PGT broke away from the organization and took up arms. The rest of the organization joined the armed struggle in 1982 when they made their alliance with the other armed movements in the URNG.[38]

ARMED REVOLUTIONARY STRUGGLE AND TRANSITION TO DEMOCRACY IN THE THIRD PHASE (1985–1996)

In 1982 when Efraín Ríos Montt came to power in a military coup, the tide began to turn against the guerrilla organizations. Ríos Montt, largely through an explicit campaign of state terror, managed to achieve a military victory over the guerrilla organizations that was more or less complete by 1985.[39] Despite great casualties and a decisive military defeat, the URNG and all of its member organizations managed to survive as organizations. This outcome stands in contrast to the complete dissolution of guerrilla organizations at the end of the first phase.

[35] For a discussion of the Indian question by the EGP leadership, see _Articles from the Compañero: The International Magazine of Guatemala's Guerrilla Army of the Poor_ (San Francisco: Solidarity Publications, 1982), 17–26.

[36] Concerned Guatemala Scholars, _Dare to Struggle_, 19–21; Longman, _Latin American Political Movements_, 45.

[37] Wickham-Crowley, Guerrillas, 217, 289; Jonas, Battle, 138; Concerned Guatemala Scholars, Dare to Struggle, 19–21; Longman, _Latin American Political Movements_, 145.

[38] Wickham-Crowley, _Guerrillas_, 224; Barry and Preusch, _The Central American Fact Book_, 233; Jonas, _Battle_, 138.

[39] Wickham-Crowley, _Guerrillas_, 289–290.

At the same time that the disparate Guatemalan guerrilla organizations were forging a new and unified front, the threat of US intervention in Central America (particularly in Nicaragua) prompted other Latin American nations to initiate the beginnings of a peace process that would eventually lead to a transition to civil society for armed revolutionary movements in Guatemala. Although the efforts of Colombia, Mexico, Panama, and Venezuela (the Contadora Group) did not result in a peace settlement, they did open up the possibility for negotiation and an eventual transition to democracy.[40]

While the leadership of the URNG resolved its sectarian struggles in the early 1980s, it was also precisely at this time that it began to lose the military battle with the Guatemalan armed forces.[41] The guerrillas could not have anticipated the genocidal strategy of General Fernando Romeo Lucas García (1978–1982). The more organized and deadly counterinsurgency strategy of Ríos Montt was even more devastating – to both the guerrilla forces and the civilian population. The guerrillas failed to offer any real protection to the indigenous population of the highlands during this period.[42] Despite the fact that the URNG was unable to effectively counter the military offensive of the state, it was not completely defeated in a political sense. It was able to survive as an organization, which had the effect of denying the Guatemalan military a victory as well. In accordance with Guevara's theory of revolutionary warfare, the ability of the guerrillas to resist annihilation constituted its own kind of victory through attrition.

Nevertheless by the mid-1980s, it had become clear that a continuation of the struggle through combat would be extraordinarily costly for the rural civilian population. At the same time, the 1985 democratic election of Vinicio Cerezo presented an opportunity to seek legitimacy through incorporation into civil society.[43]

Internal Structure during the Third Phase (1985–1996)

According to most scholars, the internal cohesion of the URNG began to fracture by 1983 in response to the genocidal campaign of Efraín Ríos

---

[40] Dario Moreno, *The Struggle for Peace in Central America* (Gainesville: University Press of Florida, 1994).

[41] Susanne Jonas, *Of Centaurs and Doves: Guatemala's Peace Process* (Boulder, CO: Westview Press, 2000), 24.

[42] Jonas, *Of Centaurs*, 24, 29.   [43] Jonas, *Of Centaurs*, 30.

Montt. The surviving core of the URNG (which was made up of the FAR, the EGP, the ORPA, and the PGT) was splintered and scattered.[44] The question of whether to continue the strategy of armed struggle given the humanitarian costs was a divisive issue. The general commanders of each of the four groups moved permanently to Mexico City in 1984, and the remaining members of the movement retreated to remote parts of Guatemala or other parts of Mexico.[45]

The guerrillas remained physically splintered and by all accounts divided over the question of whether to pursue a military solution. And in 1984, Mario Payeras split from the EGP, forming a dissident group within the URNG (called *el contingente* and then later the *Octubre Revolucionario*) that criticized the centralized vertical structure of the EGP as well as the continuance of a strictly military strategy. The PGT had lost power and influence within the URNG by the 1980s, but it too gave rise to a similar splinter organization at the same time, called the *PGT 6 de enero*. After 1985, individuals within the leadership of all four of the constituent groups of the URNG consistently pressed the guerrillas to seek a political solution. While the insistence on a vertical military hierarchy and intolerance for internal debate were perceived as necessary conditions for the preservation of physical security, the rigid military structure of the URNG during this period problematized the transition to a political party later on.[46]

While refusing to demobilize, and maintaining adherence to the possibility of a military victory, the URNG cautiously pursued a political strategy (while continuing to exert military pressure) after 1986. Informal meetings between the guerrilla leadership, the Cerezo administration, and international negotiators took place in Costa Rica and in Spain in 1986. Although these talks prompted the Guatemalan military to assassinate the Guatemalan ambassador to Spain, Vinicio Cerezo was not deterred. Cerezo's National Reconciliation Commission (CNR)[47] sponsored its first formal talks in Oslo in 1990.

---

[44] Saul Landau, *The Guerrilla Wars of Central America: Nicaragua, El Salvador and Guatemala* (New York: St. Martin's Press, 1993), 191.

[45] Landau, *The Guerrilla Wars*, 191; Dirk Kruijt, *Guerrillas: War and Peace in Central America* (New York: Zed Books, 2008), 144–145.

[46] Anna Vinegrad, "From Guerrillas to Politicians: The Transition of the Guatemalan Revolutionary Movement in Historical and Comparative Perspective," in *Guatemala after the Peace Accords*, ed. by Rachel Seider. London: Institute of Latin American Studies, University of London, 1998), 217.

[47] *Comisión Nacional de Reconciliación*

These were followed by a series of bilateral conferences between the URNG and various political constituencies.[48] Unlike neighboring El Salvador, factions within both the military and the URNG were prepared to continue fighting for a decade or more if a political solution did not emerge.

Civilian government appointees, members of the armed forces, and the four members of the URNG command and their advisers carried out the formal negotiations, which took six full years.[49] At the end of 1996, the final peace accord was signed. Because of an ill-advised kidnapping by ORPA in October 1996, the formal transition of the URNG to a political party was delayed until 1999.[50]

Mobilization Strategy during the Third Phase (1985–1996)

The third phase was a period of decline and transition for the URNG. The number of active armed militants never returned to the earlier high point before the genocide. Although they did recuperate to some extent and they were able to exert new military initiatives by the 1990s, they completely abandoned the effort to mobilize urban popular sectors and a broad base of auxiliary support forces. In other words, they abandoned the goal of mass insurrection while they transitioned toward a political solution. Their connections to the broader popular movement were stressed, with an emphasis on broad shared (class-based) interests. While they were formally connected to the popular movement, and after 1985 to a broad range of civil society, and while they were formally linked with various civil society constituencies during the period of negotiations (1990–1996), they were often criticized for being out of touch with the broader interests of poor, particularly indigenous Guatemalans. The EGP was more directly connected to the popular movement and was given the charge of developing solidarity with the base, while ORPA had the primary organizational authority to maintain an active military resistance. Despite some of the problems inherent in maintaining a mobilized constituency while the military conflict was winding down, ORPA did successfully negotiate a series of accords that addressed particular social problems that were articulated by the base, including racism.[51]

---

[48] Kruijt, *Guerrillas*, 144–145. [49] Kruijt, *Guerrillas*, 150.
[50] Vineyard, "From Guerrillas to Politicians," 220–224; Kruijt, *Guerrillas*, 150.
[51] Interview, Ing. Raul Molina, Guatemala City, August 14, 1999.

Ideology during the Third Phase (1985–1996)

The evolving ideology of the guerrilla movement in the context of the transition to democracy is, of course, enmeshed in the changing social and political context. As explained earlier, the election of Vinicio Cerezo came at a time of reflection for the guerrilla movement, and it also provided a unique and somewhat risky opportunity. The leadership of the URNG was hesitant to make a quick transition to civil society, for both ideological and pragmatic reasons. The experience of the late 1960s was a lesson in distrust. And although many things were changing within the Guatemalan military and Guatemalan society as whole, the leadership was still dealing with a reactionary and extremely racist political and military establishment. While ideological evolution was necessary and also somewhat organic given the changing dynamics of the popular movement and the transition of the popular movement into civil society, these transitions created a number of tensions within the armed movement.

"POPULAR" VS. "ETHNIC" POLITICS

The politics of transition in Guatemala took place in a much broader context in which the Cold War was ending, and the "popular revolutionary" struggles were confronted with the necessity of integrating into civil society. Scholars sometimes refer to this shifting terrain and the new forms of popular mobilization that emerged as "New Social Movements." New Social Movements generally emphasize a more postmodern and subjective politics of identity over the class-based politics of absolute opposition to hegemonic states that characterized the earlier period.[52]

In Guatemala, the ethnic reality of the nation created a natural tension between the popular movement (and especially the popular revolutionary struggle) and the needs and desires of the most obvious protagonists or allies of a revolutionary movement – the Maya majority. By the beginning of the second phase, the guerrilla movements had reconsidered the role of indigenous peasants in the struggle. By 1979, the EGP viewed indigenous militants as important revolutionary allies, and the ORPA defined the indigenous peasants as the protagonists of revolutionary struggle in Guatemala.[53] Despite these shifts, indigenous leaders/commanders, especially at the national level, were almost nonexistent, and the official

[52] A fuller discussion of "New Social Movements" can be found in Chapter 7.
[53] Interview, Molina.

ideology of the URNG, although it acknowledged the problems of racism, was firmly based in a Western Marxist analysis of social class.

At the same time, increasing numbers of indigenous peasants were becoming integrated into the global economy of agro-export (proletarianized) and a new class of highly educated Maya came of age and forged new ethnic political movements that emphasized and prioritized ethnicity as the primary social category. These organizations eventually constituted a Pan-Maya movement by the late 1980s. There was (and still is) some overt ideological conflict between the so-called popular struggle and the new Maya politics that had to be navigated at the same time that the URNG was moving toward a political (as opposed to a military) solution, and the required acceptance of a liberal democratic model that this implied.

CONCLUSIONS

The story of armed struggle in Guatemala during this era is both distinct from the other Caribbean Revolutionary movements and deeply ingrained in that regional experience. The Guatemalan revolutionaries of the MR-13 were motivated by the Cuban example, as well as their own history of reformist revolution under Juan José Arevalo and Jacobo Arbenz. They were well-versed in Marxist analysis, but they were not unaware of the ethnic reality of their country. The counterinsurgent response of the Guatemalan state in many ways mirrored the state terror of El Salvador and the corruption of Nicaragua, but the genocidal proportions of the scorched earth campaign of Ríos Montt went beyond what other military dictators imposed. The importance of finding meaning in this struggle and the sacrifice that it required is echoed in the other cases studied here.

Suggested Reading

Garrard-Burnett, Virginia. *Terror in the Land of the Holy Spirit*. New York: Oxford University Press, 2010.

Grandin, Greg. *Blood of Guatemala: A History of Race and Nation*. Durham, NC: Duke University Press, 2000.

Jonas, Susanne. *Of Centaurs and Doves: Guatemala's Peace Process*. Boulder, CO: Westview Press, 2000.

May, Rachel. *Terror in the Countryside*. Athens: Ohio University Press, 2001.

Menchú, Rigoberta, *I, Rigoberta Menchú*. Ed. Elisabeth Burgos-Debray. Trans. Ann Wright. London: Verso Editions, 1984.

Nelson, Diane. *A Finger in the Wound: A Body Politics in Quincentennial Guatemala*. Berkeley: University of California Press, 1999.

Schirmer, Jennifer. *The Guatemalan Military Project: A Violence Called Democracy*. Philadelphia: University of Pennsylvania Press, 1998.
Wilkinson, Daniel. *Silence on the Mountain: Stories of Terror, Betrayal, and Forgetting in Guatemala*. Durham, NC: Duke University Press, 2002.

Websites

Centro de Documentación de los Movimientos Armados (CEDEMA)
   www.cedema.org/?ver=portada
Official Website for the UNRG-Maiz
   www.urng-maiz.org.gt/new/drupal/node/8

Films

Granito: How to Nail a Dictator (2012)
Mayan Renaissance (2012)
Men with Guns (1997)
Reparando (2010)
When the Mountains Tremble (1984)

3

Armed Revolutionary Struggle in El Salvador

El Salvador had been the scene of popular revolutionary mobilization and violent reactionary politics since the 1920s. The smallest country in Central America was also one of the most economically and socially unequal, with a recalcitrant oligarchy and a tradition of brutal retaliation against any challenges to the social order. Agustín Farabundo Martí, the namesake of one of the most successful armed revolutionary movements in Latin America,[1] was born into a middle-class family in a small farming community in La Libertad in 1893. He attended Catholic schools until he entered the national University of El Salvador where he studied political science and law. He eventually left the university and took up labor and popular organizing. He was a founding member of the Communist Party of El Salvador, and he was the organizer of the 1932 peasant uprising that would serve as a precursor to the armed revolutionary movement of the Cold War era that took his name.[2] That 1932 peasant uprising provoked a bloody massacre – known as *La Matanza*, or "the massacre" – of mostly indigenous peasants and activists. It was also in the aftermath of La Matanza that Farabundo Martí was captured and killed.[3]

---

[1] Although the FMLN never took power through armed force, it is nonetheless considered to be a successful revolutionary group, given the high level of mobilization and insurrectionary potential it achieved between 1979 and 1981, as well as its military achievements and control of territory. See Cynthia McClintock, *Revolutionary Movements in Latin America, El Salvador's FMLN and Peru's Shining Path* (Washington, DC: US Institute of Peace, 1998).

[2] Jorge Arias Gómez, *Farabundo Martí* (San Salvador: Ocean Sur, 2010).

[3] Thomas Anderson, *Matanza* (Willimantic, CT: Curbstone Press, 1995).

The Communist Party of El Salvador (PCS)[4] was founded in March 1930 by Farabundo Martí and the well-known Salvadoran labor leader and revolutionary Miguel Mármol, among others. The party was affiliated with the Communist International and was officially recognized as a legal political party by the reformist government of Arturo Araujo before the military strongman Maximiliano Hernández Martínez deposed that government in December 1931. After La Matanza (1932), the PCS operated mostly clandestinely until the 1960s. It was also chastised by the Soviet Union for inspiring and organizing the peasant insurrection. Consequently it was hesitant to support an armed guerrilla strategy, even after the Cuban Revolution. Although it maintained a continuous presence in the country between 1930 and 1970, it was for most of this period a skeletal operation working underground with union activists and proletarianized labor.[5]

In the decades that followed La Matanza, the Salvadoran economy became increasingly modernized and connected to the global economy, particularly with the United States. And the landed elites became increasingly entrenched in a reactionary protectionist mode. The armed forces of El Salvador, which traditionally had protected the economic interests of the oligarchy, became more autonomous and ideological over the course of the mid-twentieth century. Because of economic modernization and globalization, a nascent middle class emerged. This middle class was viewed as inherently threatening by both the traditional elites and the military. During the 1950s, El Salvador was affected by both the growth in middle-class political parties and the growing economic and political influence of the United States. The Cold War and the McCarthy era paranoia in the United States sparked an outsized brand of anticommunist sentiment that influenced US policy toward Central America even before the Cuban Revolution. Within El Salvador, moderate middle-class parties emerged that competed with the traditional economic elites, but any movement toward social reform was effectively blocked. The US presence in El Salvador was significant by the 1960s, consolidating a virulent intolerance for any hint of socialist rhetoric. Throughout this period the alliance between the military and the oligarchy controlled national politics through corruption and fraud, creating strong cynicism and discontent among the middle class and the poor majority.[6]

---

[4] *Partido Comunista del Salvador*
[5] Roque Dalton, *Miguel Mármol* (Willimantic, CT: Curbstone Press: 1982), 139–168.
[6] Robert Armstrong and Janet Shenk, *El Salvador: The Face of Revolution* (Boston MA: Southend Press, 1982), 33–58.

At the same time the Catholic Church in El Salvador was particularly influenced by liberation theology and the growth of Christian Base Communities (CEBs).[7] The growing intolerance of the reactionary elites practically forced the Church into an alliance with the opposition.[8]

As was the case in the rest of the region, the Church was undergoing a radical transformation in the years after the Second Vatican Council concluded its meetings in 1965. The overarching purpose of "Vatican II" was to make the modern Church more relevant to Catholics. This was especially important in Latin America because it was and remains the largest concentration of Catholics in the world, and the Latin American Church had been isolated from Rome for hundreds of years after its inception in the sixteenth century. The movement to modernize and fortify the Latin American Church had been underway for more than a decade by the time Vatican II concluded. A shortage of priests in the region led many religious orders to send European missionaries to Latin America, beginning in the 1950s. In El Salvador a generation of Jesuit novitiates (young men, sometimes adolescents, who intended to become Jesuit priests) arrived in El Salvador in the 1950s and 1960s. These young men came of age and became priests in the highly unequal and repressive society that defined El Salvador. The inequalities and injustices of this "new world" had an impact on how these priests interpreted and carried out the mandates of Vatican II. Not enough priests were available to provide pastoral care to the large Catholic population; as a result, Salvadoran priests (like their other Latin American counterparts) encouraged and trained laypeople to run smaller "base communities" within the churches. These CEBs engaged in Bible study and prayer, but they were also called to social action. Eventually these biblical interpretations of the poor (in El Salvador and elsewhere in Latin America) led to the "theology of liberation." When reading and analyzing the Bible, poor people from Latin America were particularly attuned to the humble origins of Jesus, and the close connections between the life of Jesus and poor people. Their attention was drawn to Jesus's words regarding poverty and social injustice. These interpretations borne of hardship eventually "filtered up" into the Latin American Church hierarchy, which led to strong statements in support of social justice and the poor at the Latin American Bishop's Conference in Medellin, Colombia, in 1968.

---

[7] *Comunidades Eclesiales de Base*
[8] Penny Lernoux, *Cry of the People* (New York: Doubleday, 1980).

This shift of the Latin American Church created much division among the Church hierarchy, especially in El Salvador where the bishops were fairly evenly divided between those who were influenced by liberation theology and those who were opposed to the "politicization" of the Church and preferred to maintain the Church's long and deep connections with Salvadoran elites. Oscar Romero was appointed as the archbishop of San Salvador in February 1977. He had been an ordained priest for thirty-five years at that time, and he had a reputation for being theologically conservative, and apolitical. Over the course of his time as archbishop he was "converted" to a position of solidarity with the poor and oppressed. This was especially true as the violence and atrocities of the Salvadoran military intensified in the late 1970s. While maintaining a strict position of pacifism, Romero spoke out regularly in support of the poor, and he denounced the violent human rights abuses of the military government as well as the profound social injustices of Salvadoran society. He was assassinated by a government-connected death squad on March 23, 1980, while saying mass. Pope Francis beatified him in 2015. And he remains a potent symbol of the cause for justice that lay underneath the civil war in El Salvador.

El Salvador's first phase of revolutionary violence coincides roughly with Guatemala's second phase, thus putting Guatemala almost a decade ahead of El Salvador by the time an armed movement is launched. From 1969 to 1980 (the first phase), various groups within the popular struggle launched more than five attempts at armed revolutionary struggle before coming together under the banner of the Farabundo Martí National Liberation Front (FMLN) in 1980. Between 1980 and 1989 (the second phase), the FMLN was able to launch an aggressive campaign to take power in El Salvador, culminating in the siege of San Salvador (the "Final Offensive") in November 1989. After this siege ultimately failed and the Soviet Union collapsed, the Salvadoran government and the FMLN entered into serious negotiations to end the conflict (1989–1992 – the third phase). These talks resulted in the transition of the FMLN into a civilian political party by the mid-1990s.

ARMED REVOLUTIONARY STRUGGLE IN THE FIRST PHASE (1969–1980)

The comparative delay in the initiation of armed struggle in El Salvador was due in part to the historic influence of the Communist Party of El Salvador (PCS). During the 1960s the PCS was still closely tied to the Soviet Union, and as such it opposed a Cuban-style revolution and guerrilla warfare. In 1963 it briefly experimented with a political-military operation called the United Front of Military action (FUAR),[9] which was quickly abandoned in favor of a perceived political opening through electoral politics.[10] During the 1960s the PCS still had a very small membership base, mostly in the national University of El Salvador. Although it was operating clandestinely at the time, there was considerable overlap in membership with the leftist Democratic Nationalist Union (UDN),[11] which participated in electoral politics during the 1960s.[12] The PCS finally took up arms again in 1977. Prior to that in 1970 – because the PCS had decided against armed struggle – its leader, Salvador Cayetano Carpio, left the party to form a new revolutionary organization that would engage a military strategy. Carpio's Popular Liberation Force (FPL)[13] was eventually allied with a broad popular front organization, the Popular Revolutionary Bloc (BPR)[14] in 1975.

Soon after Carpio left the PCS in 1970, another group of dissidents withdrew from the Communist Party and formed an alliance with other Leftist allies, initially calling themselves "The Group" (*El Grupo*). The Group eventually became the Peoples' Revolutionary Army (ERP)[15] in 1972. In 1975 Roque Dalton, the famed revolutionary poet, who had returned from exile in the early 1970s to join the struggle, was falsely accused by the ERP of being an agent of the CIA. Dalton had ideological differences with the leadership of the ERP, particularly Joaquín Villalobos, and Dalton paid for these disagreements with his life. Many in the movement viewed Roque Dalton's murder as intolerable. Many militants, including leadership, withdrew from the ERP in 1975 to create the National Resistance (RN).[16] The RN created a broad popular front, which then created a secondary guerrilla wing called the Armed Forces of National Resistance (FARN).[17]

The fifth armed revolutionary movement in El Salvador during this first phase was the Revolutionary Party of Central American Workers (PRTC).[18] The PRTC was founded in San José (Costa Rica) in 1975 by an international group of Central American revolutionaries. The founding

[9] *Frente Unido de Acción Revoucionaria*
[10] The head of the FUAR, Shafick Jorge Handal, was also arrested.
[11] *Unión Democrática Nacionalista*
[12] The UDN eventually allied itself with the FMLN in the 1980s.
[13] *Fuerzas Populares de Liberación*   [14] *Bloque Popular Revolucionario*
[15] *Ejército Revolucionario del Pueblo*   [16] *Resistencia Nacional*
[17] *Fuerzas Armadas de Resistencia Nacional*
[18] *Partido Revolucionario de Trabajadores de Centroamérica*

members of the PRTC included dissidents from the ERP and the RN, as well as other mostly university-based militants from El Salvador. Interestingly some of the founding members of the PRTC went on to assume leadership positions within the Revolutionary Organization of the People in Arms (ORPA) in Guatemala.

After numerous failed attempts at unity in the late 1970s when popular unrest was at its height, these five armed revolutionary movements (PCS, FPL, ERP, RN/FARN, and PRTC) came together in 1980 to form the FMLN.[19]

Internal Structure during the First Phase (1969–1980)

The Communist International created the PCS in the late 1920s, and its internal structure maintained the traditional form of Soviet-inspired and recognized communist parties throughout the middle of the first phase. It was led by a secretary general and was organized into cadres (clandestine cells). The PCS was a relatively small organization throughout the first and second phases. It assumed military operations only during a period of mass insurrection in 1977.

The FPL was the political-military organization founded by Salvador Cayetano Carpio, who left the PCS in protest over its Soviet-influenced strategy and refusal to take up arms. After 1975 the political organizing activities of the FPL were handled by the BPR, while military operations were the purview of the FPL. The structural organization was influenced by Carpio's background as the former secretary general for the PCS. It mirrored the Communist Party's hierarchical structure of organized cadres.

The ERP was also a more remote offshoot of the PCS. The predecessor of the ERP, El Grupo, was made up of younger dissidents of the PCS along with militants coming from Christian Youth and the New Left.[20] The ERP was originally more loosely organized than the other guerrilla groups, and its leadership and membership were mostly younger and drawn from the middle class. Its founders came disproportionately from the Christian Democratic Party (PDC)[21] rather than the Communist Party. Eventually it adopted a foquista strategy. Its integration with the popular movement was minimal.

---

[19] *Frente Farabundo Martí de la Liberación Nacional.* See Tommy Sue Montgomery, *Revolution in El Salvador: From Civil Strife to Civil Peace,* 2nd ed. (Boulder, CO: Westview Press, 1995).
[20] McClintock, *Revolutionary Movements,* 50.   [21] *Partido de la Democracia Cristiana*

The RN broke away from the ERP, again over the question of the role of popular mobilization (the issue that prompted the treason allegations against Roque Dalton). The RN structured itself as a popular broad front organization and then created a military wing (the FARN) as a secondary organization. While its military organization was much smaller and carried out fewer operations than did that of the FPL or the ERP, it was organized into four guerrilla fronts. The military structure was a traditional vertical hierarchy, and the broad front organization mirrored that military structure.

Dissidents from the ERP founded the precursor to the PRTC in 1973. A group of primarily Salvadoran revolutionaries that also included other Central Americans formed the Revolutionary Workers' Organization (ORT)[22] in 1973. They had clandestine cells in Costa Rica, Honduras, El Salvador, Mexico, and the United States. In 1975, under the leadership of Fabio Castillo Figueroa, the former rector of the University of El Salvador, a new Marxist-Trotskyite organization was forged out of the ORT. It held its first party congress in San José in January 1976. The PRTC was a regional organization with a prescribed directive body in every country in Central America with the exception of Nicaragua. In 1979 it created a broad front organization called the Movement for the Liberation of the People (MLP).[23] Figure 3.1 illustrates the historical evolution of the complex changing alliances between the various armed movements in El Salvador during the first phase.

Mobilization Strategy during the First Phase (1969–1980)

The PCS maintained its adherence to the Soviet strategy of organizing within urban trade unions and forging (clandestine) electoral alliances with more moderate Leftist political parties. It participated in the elections of both 1972 and 1977. Although it remained illegal and clandestine throughout the first phase and was relatively small (200 members in 1972), it had considerable overlap with legal popular organizations and political parties and extensive connections (and the resources that this implied) with the Soviet Union. Its mobilization strategy during this first phase was based primarily within the university and was broadly reliant upon its alliances with the center-left political coalitions.

---

[22] *Organización Revolucionaria de Trabajadores*
[23] *Movimiento de Liberación del Pueblo*. Centro de Documentación de Movimientos Armadas, "En Que Contexto Surge el PRTC," www.cedema.org/ver.php?id=1554.

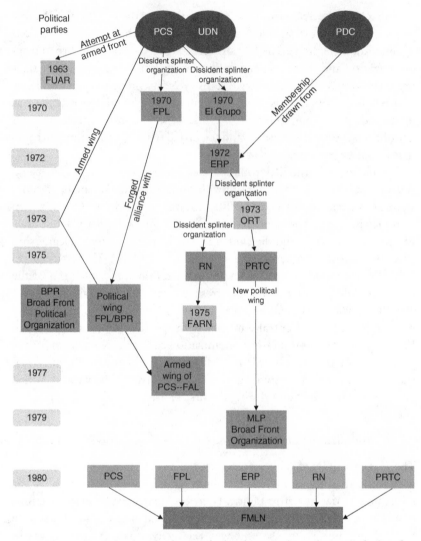

FIGURE 3.1 Organizational chart of the historical evolution of the five organizations making up the FMLN

Salvador Carpio's Popular Liberation front worked intensively with workers and peasants to create a broad popular coalition. Carpio had been the secretary general of the Communist Party before he split to create an armed movement. Modeling themselves after the Communists, they forged an alliance with the BPR in 1975. This alliance was illustrative of their popular mobilization strategy. The BPR was the largest popular front organization in the country by the late 1970s.

The ERP was led by Joaquín Villalobos and was composed of younger and more middle-class revolutionaries than either the PCS or the FPL. They were inclined toward a foquista strategy and believed that high-profile military actions would be the key to mobilizing a mass insurrection. They were less interested in popular organizing than the FPL and were comparatively less successful at building alliances with the popular movement. The exclusive focus on military action (and the neglect of a more popular strategy) was precisely what prompted the criticism of Roque Dalton, who was a strong advocate for a more popular and political approach.

Since the founding leaders of the RN were motivated by their allegiance to Dalton, they were sympathetic to Dalton's criticism of the military focus of the ERP. They consequently emphasized popular organizing. And in fact their "popular front" (RN) was the primary organization, and the military arm of the RN – the FARN – was formed afterward and was secondary to the popular front organization.

The PRTC was the smallest of the organizations that made up the FMLN. It was informed by its internationalist Trotskyite ideology and attempted to organize separate clandestine cadres among peasants, workers, and intellectuals in each of the countries of Central America (except for Nicaragua) in the spirit of internationalism. Its actual organizing capability was comparatively small.

Ideology during the First Phase (1969–1980)

The ideology of the PCS was Soviet-line communism. Following the direction and lead of the Soviet leadership, it favored a measured and conciliatory approach toward electoral politics as an intermediate strategy. The Communist International historically pushed affiliated communist parties to pursue a strategy that modeled the Bolshevik Revolution in Russia. In both Russia and China, the Communist revolutionaries were only successful after a precursor "bourgeois" revolution. The Cuban Revolution did not follow this model. The 26th of July Movement, which was mostly a campesino-based movement overthrew Batista's dictatorship without an intermediary "liberal" revolution. The PCS was one of the most well-established Soviet-aligned communist parties in Latin America, and consequently it favored the approach of forging electoral alliances with liberal political parties to oppose the reactionary right as a necessary precursor to an armed communist revolution. Consequently it did not engage in armed combat until after 1977 when it created the Armed Forces for Liberation (FAL).[24]

The splinter organization FPL was influenced by its founder Salvador Carpio's long history with the PCS. Carpio was a committed and orthodox Marxist who had been critical of the Cuban foquista model. He instead advocated for a prolonged people's war, modeled on those in China and Vietnam. The Marxist-Leninist ideology of the FPL informed its extensive organizing work among workers and peasants.

The other group that splintered away from the PCS was the ERP, and it was inspired by the Cuban example. Inasmuch as it adhered to any ideology it was Guevara's foquismo. It eschewed popular education and formation and pursued an almost entirely military strategy in the countryside.

The ideology of the RN, a splinter group of the ERP, was also cast in opposition to the orthodox Soviet Marxism of the PCS, but it (in contrast to the ERP) maintained a more rigidly traditional Marxist-Leninist stance. Its mass organizing work was referred to as the creation of a true vanguard party. Nevertheless it was firmly committed to armed insurrection as well.

The PRTC was started by an older generation of committed Marxists as an international organization committed to Trotskyism. It organized disparate cells in Costa Rica, Guatemala, Honduras, and El Salvador. It was the smallest and youngest organization to join the FMLN, and it was required to abandon its internationalism as a condition of its inclusion in the FMLN in 1980.

The ideological differences among these various revolutionary movements seem in retrospect to be trivial and irrelevant, but they were typical of the debates and conflicts that existed between dogmatic Leftist revolutionaries of the era. These differences were the subject of one of Roque Dalton's most famous poems, "Decires," or "Sayings," where he laments that he would not want "life to pass him by" while he argued over Marxism-Leninism, all the while forgetting that he had the tools of revolution already at his disposal.

---

[24] *Fuerzas Armadas para la Liberación*

ARMED REVOLUTIONARY STRUGGLE IN THE SECOND PHASE (1980–1989)

As was the case in Guatemala in the 1960s, the ideological rigidity of the Salvadoran political-military organizations of the first phase impeded unity and solidarity between factions, for at least a time. After a brutal massacre in Plaza Libertad in February 1977, the PCS created its first armed militias – the Armed Forces for Liberation (FAR) – and began to seek reunification with the RN and the FPL. The Salvadoran military took power in a coup d'etat in October 1979 and eliminated all semblance of democratic politics. After this coup, the PCS, along with the RN and the FPL, created a joint coordinating body called the Revolutionary Coordination of the Masses (CRM).[25] The decision to put aside ideological and sectarian differences was in part a response to the Sandinista victory in Nicaragua. It also reflected the general recognition that El Salvador was in fact already poised for mass insurrection. The CRM was the manifestation of unity between the mass organizations (not yet the military organizations) of these three guerrilla groups, and the ERP was still not included because it did not have a mass organization. At the end of May 1980, the ERP joined together with the affiliated military organizations of the CRM (the PCS, FPL, and RN/FARN) to found the Unified Revolutionary Directorate (DRU).[26]

The political situation had devolved into chaos by mid-1980. In March 1980 the government announced a state of emergency (*estado de sitio*), and the level and intensity of state-sponsored terror increased dramatically, culminating in the murder of Archbishop Oscar Romero on March 24. The potential (security) benefits for solidarity increased accordingly. In April 1980 the broad front political organization of the CRM had joined with a center-left coalition that included all of the mass popular organizations, middle-class political parties, trade unions, the National University, and the Catholic Church. This new unified mass organization was called the Revolutionary Democratic Front (FDR).[27] The leadership of the FDR was composed of three members of the political directorate from each of the four political-military organizations represented (PCS, FPL, ERP, and RN). They proclaimed in their founding manifesto that they would have one leadership, one military plan, one

[25] *Coordinación Revolucionaria de las Masas* – Montgomery, Revolution in El Salvador, 105.

[26] *Dirección Revolucionaria Unida*

[27] *Frente Democrático Revolucionario*. Montgomery, *Revolution in El Salvador*, 111.

command, and one political line. The full realization of this unity occurred on October 10, 1980 with the formation of the *Frente Farabundo Martí de Liberación Nacional,* or the FMLN. The RN, which had withdrawn from the DRU during the summer, rejoined the union (and the FMLN) in November; in December 1980 the PRTC and its armed wing, the ERTC,[28] joined with the FMLN. In January 1981 the FMLN launched its first major offensive. And in 1989, it organized its second and last major national offensive.

Internal Structure during the Second Phase (1980–1989)

Although the FMLN was successfully unified under a coalition command of leadership from all five of the guerrilla member organizations, its structure remained complex including, in addition to the five military organizations, no fewer than a dozen popular and youth organizations and coalitions. The military structure of the FMLN was constrained by the necessities of combat. Its army was called the Revolutionary Popular Army (EPR).[29] In addition to the EPR, the FMLN was composed of the "militia," which referred to lightly armed peasants and workers who acted as military auxiliaries, providing a popular base of military support for the regular army, as well as the "Popular Neighborhood Committees,"[30] which were organized as cells at the block or zone level. The popular committees had responsibility for stockpiling food and other supplies and providing logistical support. They were also responsible for mass organizing and popular education. The internal differences between the various founding organizations of the FMLN were mostly overlooked rather than resolved, but eventually the political structure of the FMLN evolved into a fairly democratic one that encompassed the participation of a broad spectrum of Salvadoran society. This helps explain the relatively quick transition to a political party as well as the later electoral successes of the FMLN.

After the FMLN was founded in 1980, there was an immediate desire to provoke a mass insurrection such as the one that preceded the Sandinista victory in Nicaragua. Preparations for a general offensive began almost immediately, and on January 10, 1981, it was launched. Two towns fell to the FMLN within hours, and the citizens of several other towns and areas of San Salvador rose up in support of the FMLN.

---

[28] *Ejército Revolucionario de los Trabajadores Centroamericanos*
[29] *Ejército Revolucionario Popular*   [30] *Comités populares de base*

But within days the FMLN fronts were forced to retreat, and the offensive failed. The failure of the first offensive was due to a lack of coordination between the various member organizations of the FMLN.

Despite the ultimate failure, the 1981 offensive had a mixed impact on the overall conflict. The US government (under the leadership of the out-going administration of Jimmy Carter) supplied the Salvadoran army with a significant increase in military aid and technical assistance, which increased again during the Ronald Reagan administration. The FMLN, despite its failure, was inspired by the offensive. It gained strength and numbers in many parts of the country. By the end of 1981 it also restruc-tured its overall organization in such a way that it could make unified decisions. The level of popular support for the FMLN increased substan-tially in the months preceding the offensive, and afterward as well. The overall impact was intensification of the conflict and of the violent suppression of all popular opposition to the military dictatorship.[31]

Mobilization Strategy during the Second Phase (1980–1989)

After the military offensive of January 1981 failed, there was some dis-agreement as to what the strategy of the FMLN should be, but it was generally agreed that a military victory brought through mass insurrection was still possible. It withdrew from the cities and worked on building up the size of its regular army (the EPR) in the zones where it had the most potential. By the middle of the decade it had forced the Salvadoran army out of roughly 25 percent of the country, effectively controlling that territory. In the early years of the 1980s the emphasis on military strength was accompanied by a political strategy that involved attempting to mobilize the masses for an insurrectionary uprising. Because state-sponsored terror was only intensified during this period, and US support created a more effective and more violent counterinsurgency operation, the popular taste for insurrection waned over time despite its organizing efforts.

In 1984 the FMLN changed its strategy to the Vietnamese approach of a prolonged people's war, long advocated by the FPL. By this time the US government was providing airplanes and other material support that allowed the Salvadoran military to launch significant air attacks. The large guerrilla battalions of the previous era were particularly vulnerable. The strategy of the FMLN was modified, and it began to focus on the

---

[31] Montgomery, *Revolution in El Salvador*, 112–133.

harassment and sabotage of the military with smaller bands of guerrilla fighters. At the same time the FMLN hoped for a military victory by attrition. More moderate elements within the party were simultaneously mobilizing a popular political base and preparing for a possible political solution. As was the case in Guatemala somewhat later, the continued military mobilization of the FMLN was thought to be an important component of the strategy of forcing the government to the negotiating table and strengthening the position of the FMLN once it got there. When a proposal to have the FMLN participate in the 1989 elections was rejected by the government, the FMLN made plans to launch its second "final offensive."

Ideology during the Second Phase (1980–1989)

The FMLN was firmly and explicitly committed to a democratic model; in fact this was a necessary condition of the unity that allowed for the initial formation of the FMLN. Nevertheless, the founding guerrilla organizations continued to maintain their own ideological commitments to the various brands of socialist, Marxist, Maoist, and Leninist thought that had inspired them originally. In early 1980 when the Unified Revolutionary Directorate (DRU) was formed through an alliance of the PCS, the FPL, and the RN/FARN, it originally operated by consensus, but the FPL, ERP, and PCS wanted to adopt the Leninist principle of democratic centralism and create a vanguard revolutionary party that would be led by the military commanders of the guerrilla armies. The RN initially objected to this on principle and withdrew only to rejoin the FMLN less than a month after its founding.

Earlier (in February1980) the Revolutionary Coordination of the Masses (CRM) published its political platform. The platform emphasized human rights and adherence to the Universal Declaration of Human Rights. This commitment to human rights was brought into the FMLN. The necessity of providing some protection and recourse to the victims of state-sponsored terror may have forced the issue of human rights to the center, which also forced the FMLN (like the URNG and its associated popular organizations) to a more liberal democratic position that would respect the rule of law and the legitimacy of an elected government. It also proposed the nationalization of banks as well as the major agro-export industries. It proposed major agrarian reform but promised to respect private property rights. It promised to provide access to credit for small- and medium-sized landowners and businesses and promised a broad program of social programs in housing, health, education, and culture[32]: "It is the unanimous opinion of the popular and democratic forces [of the FMLN] that only through the implementation of this platform will we be able to address the profound political and structural crisis in our country for the benefit of the Salvadoran people."[33] According to Tommie Sue Montgomery, the FMLN was increasingly ideologically flexible throughout the second phase as a result of its international recognition as a "representative political force," and the general recognition that it could eventually achieve its objectives through a negotiated political solution.[34]

ARMED REVOLUTIONARY STRUGGLE AND TRANSITION TO DEMOCRACY IN THE THIRD PHASE (1989–1992)

In November 1989 the FMLN launched its second major offensive. It was larger than the 1981 offensive, and it represented a level of cooperation and coordination among the constituent armies of the FMLN that was unprecedented in its nine-year history. The FMLN managed to hold large swaths of the city of San Salvador for two weeks, as well as seven other smaller cities. Many within the FMLN leadership hoped to spark a mass insurrection providing the necessary conditions for an outright military victory for the FMLN. The mass insurrection did not materialize, and in this sense the offensive was a failure. But many in the FMLN leadership hoped the offensive would strengthen the position of the FMLN and force the government to the negotiating table. And in this sense, the final offensive was a very useful precursor to a transition to democratic politics.

The Murder of the Jesuits and the Military Stalemate

The 1989 FMLN offensive took place in the context of the collapse of the Soviet Union, which inevitably spelled the end of US support for the terrorist regime. Underscoring the political futility of US support for the illegitimate Salvadoran regime was the unconscionable murder of six Jesuit priests, their housekeeper and her daughter by the US-trained Atlacatl Battalion.

---

[32] Comunicado del CRM/FMLN February 23, 1980, www.cedema.org/ver.php?id=3782.
[33] Coordinadora revolucionario de Masas (CRM), Plataforma Programática. www.cedema .org/ver.php?id=3782.
[34] Montgomery, *Revolution in El Salvador*, 119.

Two days after the start of the offensive, the FMLN had taken control of several large sections of San Salvador, and the Salvadoran army surrounded the Jesuit University of Central America (UCA) and placed signs at the entrances reading "No Classes Today." The UCA and the Jesuit priests who ran the university had been in conflict with the repressive military dictatorship since before the assassination of Archbishop Romero. As part of their mission to promote critical thinking about the social reality in El Salvador, they had educated a generation of citizens who were critical of the government. The president of the UCA, a Jesuit priest named Ignacio Ellacuria, had spoken out and written frequently about the brutality of the Salvadoran government and the social injustices that had provoked the armed insurgency. Several other priests at the university, most notably Jon Sobrino (who was out of the country during the 1989 offensive), Ignacio Martín Baró, and Segundo Montes were also well known for their commitment to social justice and their outspoken criticism of the state-sponsored terror of the Salvadoran military.

Because the university had been forcibly closed, the six Jesuits who lived in the Jesuit community on campus were fairly isolated. The Jesuit residence at the UCA housed seven Jesuits: Ellacuria, Sobrino, Martín Baró, and Montes, in addition to Fr. Juan Ramón Moreno, Fr. Joaquín López y López, and Fr. Amando López. All but Jon Sobrino were at home in the residence on the night of November 15, 1989. Their housekeeper, Elba Ramos, and her sixteen-year-old daughter, Celia Ramos were also sleeping at the residence that night. The two women had decided to sleep there because they deemed it safer since it was surrounded by the military; they feared getting caught in the crossfires of combat during the offensive. Shortly after midnight, a group of soldiers from the Atlacatl Battalion entered the university, made their way to the residence, and murdered the six priests and the two women. The murder of these unarmed civilians in the middle of the night was simply indefensible. It provoked a worldwide backlash against the Salvadoran regime and hastened the withdrawal of support from the United States.

The fact that an outright military victory of Salvadoran forces over the FMLN seemed an impossibility, combined with the prospect of losing US military support, meant that both parties had every reason to negotiate by the end of 1989.

Internal Structure during the Third Phase (1989–1992)

US officials met with the FMLN in early September 1991. The meeting set the stage for defining the conditions of a cease-fire. Later that month the president of El Salvador, Alfredo Cristiani, announced at the United Nations that the government and the rebels had reached an agreement to end the war. The Chapultepec Agreement was signed in Mexico City in January 1992 and was implemented on February 1 of that year. The cease-fire agreement was never broken by either side, but negotiations surrounding the end of hostilities and the transition to electoral politics continued into 1994.

The FMLN was comparatively successful at converting itself from a military organization into one of the two major political parties in El Salvador. Despite this, it did not promulgate its own presidential candidate in the 1994 election because divisions emerged between the five major factions of the FMLN over which candidate they should support. The UDN, which had traditionally been a coalition of more centrist elements, left the FMLN and joined a more moderate political party called the Democratic Convergence. The ideological differences and its regional strengths and weaknesses proved daunting for the FMLN in the early years of its transition, but eventually it emerged from these difficulties as one of the strongest Leftist political parties in the region.

Mobilization Strategy during the Third Phase (1989–1992)

To mobilize voters for the 1994 elections, the FMLN created an NGO called ASPAD that hired 300 voter registration promoters. The ASPAD promoters spent three months registering voters and gathering data. The different factions of the FMLN varied in experience and success in organizing voters. The PCS, as the most established political party that had significant prior electoral experience was the most successful, and the ERP was the least experienced and initially the least successful electoral faction of the FMLN.

Ideology during the Third Phase (1989–1992)

From the beginning of the transition, the FMLN acknowledged that it had been born from ideological diversity. Gerson Martínez, a member of the political commission of the FMLN, explained that FMLN's "adhesive force" was rooted in a common sense of political identity, not ideology. Martínez essentially rejected the idea of rigid ideological formation in a 1992 interview. He claimed for the FMLN a common political plan, based on shared ideals and a shared history and identity. First and foremost the FMLN defined its ideology as democratic and revolutionary.

It claimed in 1992 that its objective was to become *one* of the country's "main legal political forces." In the quest for this it has undoubtedly been successful.[35]

That is, while it maintained a commitment to armed insurrection and the basic Marxist principles of social justice and redistribution, Joaquin Villalobos highlighted three specific areas of ideological consensus by the end of the 1980s: (1) the Salvadoran army was incapable of achieving a military victory over the FMLN; (2) the FMLN should work to prevent and check US intervention and interference to "rescue" Salvadoran independence (economic, political, and military); and (3) it was committed to a negotiated political solution to end the war.[36] This "consensus" ideology emphasized nationalism and sovereignty over Marxism. The FMLN's commitment to a negotiated settlement evidenced an underlying commitment to liberal democracy, which was eventually borne out in its transition to a political party.

CONCLUSIONS

In El Salvador the impetus for armed rebellion was primarily a nationalist one. Guerrillas in El Salvador were responding to gross social inequalities and historical injustice in the midst of significant economic transformation (modernization toward an export-based economy and nascent globalization). As in every case study in this volume, this primarily nationalist movement was transformed by the context of the Cold War and quickly adapted to this context by adopting a range of Marxist ideologies, all of which proved to be inflexible and ultimately divisive.

The Communist Party acted as a conservative influence on the rebels. It was late in adopting armed struggle as the dominant strategy. At the point at which an armed insurgency became the dominant feature of the movement, the FMLN had aligned itself with a broad cross-section of Salvadoran society, and its vulnerability to violence of the military dictatorship informed its pragmatic commitment to the international human rights regime. This reliance on international human rights norms informed its connection to many of the principles of liberal democracy.

[35] Equipo Envio, "The FMLN from Within: Ideological Diversity, Political Unity," *Revista Envio* 33 (í 1992) UCA: Managua, Nicaragua.

[36] Joaquín Villalobos, *El Salvador: el estado actual de la guerra y sus perspectivas* (Madrid: Ediciones Revolución, 1986), 41.

The United States was heavily involved in designing and supporting counterinsurgency efforts, particularly during the Reagan years. The brutal anti-communist counterinsurgency campaigns exacted enormous human costs, but also prompted the growth of the human rights movement that pushed the FMLN toward a respect for liberal democracy, ideological diversity, and the rule of law.

The FMLN was much more organizationally tied to the popular movement than most armed revolutionary movements in the Caribbean Basin. Some of the so-called political-military organizations that made up the FMLN were forged as popular coalitions from their inception. And the level of "revolutionary" popular mobilization was higher in the more densely populated and more ethnically homogenous El Salvador than in any other country in Central America.

By the 1980s the primary question for the Salvadoran revolutionary forces was whether to seek a military solution (through outright victory or through attrition) or a political solution through negotiation. Although the FMLN was internally divided over these questions, it pursued a two-pronged approach and eventually used the threat of continuing the conflict in order to improve their negotiating position. Already by the mid-1980s, the FMLN was a more democratic political organization than the URNG in Guatemala. The FMLN more fully embraced the transition to electoral politics and also entered into negotiations with significant military strength. Consequently the FMLN has become a comparatively successful political party.

Suggested Reading

Almeida, Paul D. *Waves of Protest: Popular Struggle in El Salvador, 1925–2005*. Minneapolis: University of Minnesota Press, 2008.

Argueta, Manlio. *One Day of Life*. New York: Vintage Books (Random House), 1983.

Armstrong, Robert and Janet Shenk. *El Salvador: The Face of Revolution*. Boston: South End Press, 1982.

Dalton, Roque. *Small Hours of the Night*. Willimantic, CT: Curbstone Press. 1996.

Danner, Mark. *The Massacre at El Mozote*. New York: Vintage Books (Random House), 1994.

Grenier, Yvon. *The Emergence of Insurgency in El Salvador: Ideology and Political Will*. Pittsburgh: University of Pittsburgh Press, 1999.

Lauria-Santiago, Aldo and Leigh Binford, Eds. *Landscapes of Struggle: Politics, Society, and Community in El Salvador*. Pittsburgh: University of Pittsburgh Press, 2004.

Lernoux, Penny. *Cry of the People*. New York: Penguin, 1991.

López Vigil, José Ignacio. *Rebel Radio: The Story of El Salvador's Radio Venceremos*. Willimantic, CT: LAB and Curbstone Press, 1991.

McClintock, Cynthia. *Revolutionary Movements in Latin America: El Salvador's FMLN and Peru's Shining Path*. Washington, DC: United States Institute of Peace, 1998.

Montgomery, Tommie Sue. *Revolution in El Salvador: From Civil Strife to Civil Peace*, 2nd ed. Boulder, CO: Westview, 1994.

Teresa Tula, Maria (ed. and trans. Lynn Stephen). *Hear My Testimony*. Boston: South End Press, 1994.

Websites

Centro de Documentación de los Movimientos Armados (CEDEMA) www.cedema.org/?ver=portada

Official Site for the Frente Farabundo Martí para la Liberación Nacional www.fmln.org.sv/oficial/

Films

Carta de Morazán (2011)
Enemies of War (2000)
Guazapa: The Face of War in El Salvador (1987)
Innocent Voices (*Voces Inocentes*) (2005)
Maria's Story (1991)
Return to El Salvador (2010)
Romero (1989)
Surviving Guazapa (*Sobreviviendo Guazapa*) (2008)

4

The Armed Movement That Took Power: The Sandinista National Liberation Front in Nicaragua

One of the most significant armed revolutionary movements in Latin America is the Sandinista National Liberation Front (FSLN).[1] The confrontation between the "Sandinistas" and the dictatorial regime of the US-backed Somoza family in Nicaragua was the most publicized of the Cold War conflicts in the region. During the Cold War era the Sandinistas represented the only real alternative to the dictatorship that had governed Nicaragua from the middle of the 1930s. Eventually the Sandinistas would be the only other Latin American case of a successful armed revolutionary movement after Cuba. The FSLN was born in the 1960s in the aftermath of the Cuban Revolution, and it achieved its principal objective (overthrowing the dictatorship) in 1979.[2]

The history of Nicaragua prior to the Sandinista victory in 1979 was marked by two important factors: (1) strong interference by the United States in its domestic politics and (2) the lack of a representative and democratic system of government.

US territorial presence in Nicaragua dates back to American mercenary, William Walker's attempt to establish a slave-holding colony in the newly independent nation-state in 1856. After Walker was captured and executed, Nicaragua's geographic location attracted US officials as a potential site for building an interoceanic canal. The American

---

[1] *Frente Sandinista de Liberación Nacional*

[2] David Nolan, *La ideología sandinista y la revolución nicaragüense* (Barcelona: Ediciones 29, 1986); Timothy Wickham-Crowley, *Guerrillas and Revolution in Latin America: A Comparative Study of Insurgents and Regimes since 1956* (Princeton: Princeton University Press, 1992); Jorge Castañeda, *La Utopía desarmada: intriga, dilemas y promesa de la izquierda en América Latina* (Barcelona: Editorial Ariel, 1995).

government eventually chose Panama as the location for its canal, largely because Panama's political elite was more malleable than Nicaragua's.[3]

In 1912, at the request of then-president Adolfo Díaz, US Marines invaded the country, occupying it until 1925, when the US temporarily pulled out given relatively stable and favorable conditions. Facing the prospect of another North American intervention in 1926, the liberal peasant leader Augusto César Sandino led an armed militia (called the Army for the Defense of Nicaraguan National Sovereignty or EDSNN)[4] that fought against the conservatives and the US Marines. Sandino organized an irregular (guerrilla) army composed of laborers, peasant farmers, and small landholders. His principal objective was to repel the foreign intervention of the US military. While his ideological background was liberal,[5] his political platform had an important nationalistic component. His thoughts were not disconnected from other international processes such as the 1910 Mexican Revolution and the anarchist movement that had taken hold among the larger community of Central American urban-based workers.[6]

After six years of conflict the Marines left the country for the last time in 1933. But before the departure of the occupying forces, Anastasio Somoza García was appointed as the director of the newly created National Guard. A short time later, in February 1934 Somoza ordered the murder of Sandino and deposed the elected president, Juan Bautista Sacasa, in order to set himself up in January 1937 as the *de facto* ruler. From that point on, Somoza, a businessman with strong backing from the United States, consolidated his dictatorial control over a dependent form of capitalism based on the export of agricultural commodities, primarily coffee. Since the end of the nineteenth century, the country's economy had been based almost entirely on coffee exports. Coffee was the principal commodity until the decade of the 1950s when cotton displaced it.

One of the consequences of the growth in this monoculture export-oriented economy was the consolidation of unequal social and economic

---

[3] Panama in effect exchanged US assistance to achieve independence from Colombia for generous concessions with regard to the building of a US-controlled canal.

[4] *Ejército Defensor de la Soberanía Nacional de Nicaragua*

[5] "Liberal" in the context of twentieth-century Latin American politics refers to a commitment to the liberal ideas of the Enlightenment, specifically modern representative democracy, trade and capitalism, and "modernization."

[6] Neill Macaulay, *The Sandinista Affair* (Chicago: Quadrangle Books, 1967); Volker Wünderich, *Sandino. Una biografía política* (Managua: Instituto de Historia de Nicaragua y Centroamérica, 2009).

development. This inequality had a regional character (within Nicaragua) as well. For example, the Pacific region became much more developed and prosperous than the rest of the country. No less significant was the fact that the expansion of coffee and cotton and other export crops was achieved at the expense of basic food production. Protected by a tyrannical regime, the economic elites owned most of the land and they used it to produce cash crops for external markets.[7] As was the case in both Guatemala and El Salvador, this model of rural capitalism also contributed to the formation of a seasonal agricultural workforce that struggled for subsistence. Most campesinos were both peasant farmers and migrant wage laborers, and the system of land tenure made land ownership particularly unattainable for most Nicaraguan campesinos. There were other non-wage-earning arrangements such as sharecropping and tenant farming that also contributed to the gross inequalities in the country.[8]

The contradictions within the rural workforce also had their counterpart in the nascent industrial sector. Highly capitalized agro-business was heavily involved in agro-industrial processing, and also intimately connected to commercial and industrial capital. The large export-oriented agro-industrialists also had ties to the Somoza dictatorship, and – as a result – with the United States. Among the wealthiest economic groups in the country was the Somoza family itself.

The economic power of the Somoza dynasty in agriculture was diverse. Its presence was weak in the production of coffee, cotton, and basic grains. Nevertheless the Somozas were dominant in the production of sugar cane, irrigated rice, and tobacco and large-scale ranching. Their total investments in agriculture constituted a significant proportion of agricultural processing (mills, slaughterhouses, meat processing), and in commerce, banking, and financing. Their economic power was heavily influenced by their ability to make use of the power of the state for more than four decades. The family progressively increased its economic power until it became a monopolistic group on its own. In 1974 its fortune was calculated at $400 million.[9] Moreover, the principal economic and

---

[7] Carlos Maria Vilas, *La Revolución Sandinista* (Buenos Aires: Editorial Legasa, 1985); Eduardo Baumeister, "Estructuras productivas y reforma agraria en Nicaragua." In *La Revolución en Nicaragua*, compiled by Richard Harris, and Carlos Vilas (México D.F.: Ediciones Era, 1985), 51–80.
[8] Carlos Maria Vilas, "Las contradicciones de la transición: clases, nación y Estado en Nicaragua" *Estudios Sociales Centroamericanos* 31 (1982): 95–114.
[9] Baumeister. "Estructuras productivas."

political mechanisms of the Somoza dictatorship orbited around the demands of Washington: whether for supplies of raw materials for its market, or to intervene diplomatically in Nicaragua's negotiations with its Caribbean Basin neighbors.

THE EMERGENCE OF THE GUERRILLA

In the case of Nicaragua, there was only one significant guerrilla organization, the Sandinista National Liberation Front (FSLN) or "the Sandinistas." In this chapter we examine the evolution of the FSLN in two phases: (1) the military phase (1959–1979) and (2) the government phase after the Sandinistas successfully took power and ruled Nicaragua (1979–1989).

Internal Structure during the First (Military) Phase (1959–1979)

There are a few different versions about the exact origins of the FSLN,[10] but it is possible to identify a common narrative. Most scholars believe that there was a rebirth of armed opposition against the Somozas when they increased violent repression following the assassination of the elder dictator, Somoza García, in 1956.[11] After the founder of the dynasty was killed, his son Luís Somoza Debayle took charge of the government, while his other son (Anastasio Somoza Debayle) assumed control of the National Guard. This consolidation of dynastic rule and its expansion of direct repression against the civil population were the most important prompts for the rise of armed rebellion.

As was the case in the rest of the Caribbean Basin, the triumph of the Cuban Revolution in 1959 was also influential. In the late 1950s several student protests in the principal cities of Nicaragua expressed sympathy for Fidel Castro's revolution. These students explicitly linked the struggle against Fulgencio Batista in Cuba with opposition to the Somoza regime.

One of the principal organizations that emerged from these student protests was the Sandino Revolutionary Front (FRS)[12] founded

---

[10] Tomás Borge, *La paciente impaciencia*. Managua: Vanguardia Editores, 1989; Nolan. *La ideología sandinista*; Martí I Puig, *La izquierda revolucionaria en Centroamérica: el FSLN desde su fundación a la insurrección popular*. Barcelona: Institut de Ciencies Politiques i Socials (ICPS), 2002.

[11] Anastasio Somoza García was assassinated by the poet Rigoberto López Pérez on September 29, 1956.

[12] *Frente Revolucionario Sandino*

in March 1959 in Mexico by Latin American youth (from various countries, including Nicaragua) who were studying there. Their intention was to prepare an armed group that would enter Nicaragua across the northern border with Honduras to combat Somoza's National Guard. They expected to find old supporters of Sandino in that region. Combatants of different nationalities participated in the FRS, including Juan Moleón (Cuba), Jack Nordin and John Rigsbee (United States), Joaquín "Che" Basanta (Argentina), Santiago Mateo (El Salvador), Antonio Reu (Dominican Republic), and Héctor Zelaya (Honduras) among others. They were joined by survivors of the former army of Sandino, together with ex-members of the Nicaraguan National Guard.

Also in 1959 the National Liberation Front (FLN)[13] was formed by the ex–National Guard member Rafael Somarriba. Carlos Fonseca Amador, the future Sandinista leader, was among the original cadre of guerrillas in the FLN. These combatants centered their activities in the northern territories of Nicaragua. Their objective was to form two combatant fronts in the mountainous zone of the Segovias. This did not happen because in June 1959 the FLN was surprised by the Honduran army, which killed and wounded many, including Fonseca. Toward the end of 1959 the guerrilla army of Carlos "Chale" Haslam operated in the mountains of Matagalpa (Las Bayas, Pancasán, and El Bijao) for a brief time. Armed skirmishes also took place in Susucayán, Quilalím, and in the south of the country.

The FRS operated between November 1959 and March 1960 in a border territory that had long been disputed with Honduras. The camp's standard was the red and black flag of Sandino's old Army for the Defense of Nicaraguan National Sovereignty (EDSNN). After a bloody confrontation in February 1960 in which numerous FRS combatants were killed, the Honduran government captured several others. Following numerous student protests in Tegucigalpa requesting the liberation of the prisoners, the detained militants were released and some of them took refuge in Cuba.

From that moment on, Cuba provided substantial material and moral support to those organizations. It was in Cuba in 1960 that the FRS exiles began to establish agreements with other Nicaraguan groups, such as the Nicaraguan Revolutionary Youth (JRN), led by Tomás Borge, Silvio Mayorga, and Fonseca.[14] Other new collectives also emerged (e.g., the Patriotic Youth, the Socialist Youth, the New Nicaragua Movement[15])

[13] *Frente de Liberación Nacional*   [14] *Juventud Revolucionaria Nicaragüense*
[15] *La Juventud Patriótica, la Juventud Socialista, el Movimiento Nueva Nicaragua*

that sought to imitate the bearded men of the Cuban Revolution. The New Nicaragua Movement (MNN)[16] was born in 1961 in Cuba from the fusion of these various Nicaraguan revolutionary groups.

In 1962 Fonseca established the first school of military instruction in the Sierras de Managua. Later in 1962 the MNN and the FRS merged under the leadership of Eden Pastora and Harold Martínez; this new organization counted on substantial support from former members of Sandino's EDSNN. Sometime later this group renamed itself the Sandinista National Liberation Front (the FSLN or Sandinistas) in homage to Augusto Sandino.[17] In this way, the leaders of the FSLN sought to merge themselves with the tradition of struggle and heroism of Sandino.

During these early years the FSLN maintained a small centralized internal structure, trying to adapt itself to the strategies of Che Guevara's foquismo. At the same time Fonseca attempted to establish an urban guerrilla front in Managua; he also founded the first newspaper of the organization, known as *Trinchera* (The Trenches).

The first armed confrontations between the FSLN and the National Guard took place on the Bocay River and the River Coco in 1963. The guerrillas were defeated. By that time the group was composed of sixty men, many of whom had no military experience. After this defeat Fonseca decided to reorganize his forces and establish a new armed nuclei in the mountains. During the subsequent years, the military force of the FSLN stabilized, but in 1967, it suffered another hard setback on the Pancasán Mountain; at that time the Sandinistas lost thirteen men, including one of its founders, Silvio Mayorga.[18]

Following this latter military defeat, the surviving leaders went into exile in Cuba, Panama, and Costa Rica; from that moment on they began to consider a new strategy and a new theoretical framework for the movement. Similarly a new National Directorate was formed, composed of Carlos Fonseca, Tomás Borge, Oscar Turcios, Julio Buitrago, Ricardo Morales, Henry Ruíz, and Humberto Ortega. In 1969, the Sandinista Front Program was approved and became the new guiding manifesto for the organization. The following text communicated the foundations, proposals, and fundamental goals of the movement:

[16] *Movimiento Nueva Nicaragua*
[17] Martí I Puig. *La izquierda revolucionaria en Centroamérica.*
[18] Manlio Tirado, *La Revolución Sandinista* (México D.F.: Editorial Nuestro Tiempo, 1983).

The Sandinista Front is a military-political organization which has the strategic objective of taking political power and establishing a revolutionary government based on the worker-campesino alliance and the participation of all anti-imperialist and anti-oligarchic patriotic forces in the country.[19]

The organizational, strategic, and doctrinal re-elaboration had an impact on the organization as a whole. After this a series of criteria were established to classify the cadres, militants, sympathizers, and collaborators within the FSLN structure. *Cadres* were required to submit to a strict discipline and strong ideological preparation. At the same time a *militant* who entered the movement was considered a "legal member" whose connection to the group remained a secret to facilitate public activities. Additionally power was decentralized internally, and the various members of the National Directorate began to have greater autonomy from the central command structure.[20] The Sandinistas sought to overcome the limitations of their lack of integration in society; to this end they reorganized the armed movement on the basis of campesino-type "cells," and they also expanded their presence in urban communities, workplaces, and in Christian Base Communities.[21]

The internal structure of the FSLN was adapted to the need for clandestine growth. This strategy was characterized by an effort to avoid any confrontation with the regime while gathering supporters individually and through distinct cells dispersed throughout the country in both rural and urban areas. The internal structure of the FSLN was modified again as a result of the earthquake that devastated Managua in December 1972. The earthquake had serious economic and social consequences for the country. More than 10,000 people died in this tragedy and 75 percent of family residences in the capital city (most of them belonging to the middle- and low-income families) were destroyed. The government (the Somoza family) engaged in massive corruption and stole much of the international aid that was supposed to be used for reconstruction. This corruption very quickly alienated a broad swath of the middle and upper classes. In the face of the weak and corrupt government response to the humanitarian crisis, a broader cross section of the Nicaraguan people began to publicly

---

[19] FSLN, *Programa del Frente Sandinista de Liberación Nacional* (Managua: DPEP-FSLN, 1969).

[20] Nolan. *La ideología sandinista.*

[21] CEBs (*Comunidades Eclesiales de Base*) or Christian Base Communities were grassroots Catholic communities composed of laypeople who read the Bible and participated in community action campaigns to improve their material circumstances. Similar to El Salvador, the CEB/liberation theology movement was large and influential in Nicaragua.

demonstrate their opposition to the regime. The Somozas responded by intensifying repressive measures.

Various segments within a relatively broad sector of society began to articulate their demands and their desire for regime change. From the beginning of the 1970s the Sandinista movement had come to be seen as the most viable political alternative to the dictatorship. One factor that contributed to its consolidation was the taking of hostages in December 1974 in the house of Somoza's Minister of Agriculture José María del Castillo. After three days of negotiations, the FSLN was able to obtain the liberation of eight imprisoned Sandinistas (including the future president of Nicaragua, Daniel Ortega), $500,000 in cash, the diffusion of its message in broad media outlets, and an airplane to take refuge on the island of Cuba.[22]

Also in 1974 the Democratic Liberation Union (UDEL)[23] was formed to demand political and economic reform. This group was composed of leadership from several mainstream opposition political parties: the National Conservative Action (ANC),[24] the Movement of Liberal Constitutionalists (MLC),[25] the Independent Liberal Party (PLI),[26] the Social Christian Party (PSC),[27] and the Socialist Party of Nicaragua (PSdeN).[28] The UDEL also recruited some of the most important Nicaraguan labor unions such as the Confederation of Nicaraguan Workers (CTN)[29] and the Independent General Confederation of Workers (CGT-I).[30]

The Somoza regime intensified violent social repression that in turn resulted in increased social tension and a worsening economic crisis. Constitutional rights were then suspended, leading to more atrocities committed by the National Guard. All of this contributed to the further sullying of the spent international image of the dictatorship.

The FSLN at this time was managing emerging divisions within its ranks. These conflicts arose because of both theoretical and philosophical questions and organizational issues. This took place in a context marked by the violent Somozista repression that made communications among the principal leaders difficult (since so many of them were exiled or in prison). The divisions within the FSLN were initially born during the transition

[22] Jaime Wheelock, *Diciembre victorioso* (Managua: Editorial Nueva Nicaragua, 1982).
[23] *Unión Democrática de Liberación*   [24] *Acción Nacional Conservadora*
[25] *Movimiento Liberal Constitucionalista*   [26] *Partido Liberal Independiente*
[27] *Partido Social Cristiano*   [28] *Partido Socialista de Nicaragua*
[29] *Confederación de Trabajadores Nicaragüenses.*
[30] *Confederación General de Trabajadores-Independientes*

from a foquista strategy toward the Maoist idea of Prolonged Peoples' War (GPP)[31] in the early 1970s. Soon after this transition, some of the militants within the organization developed a new ideological line – the Proletarian Tendency (TP)[32] – which was overtly critical of the Sandinista leadership that advocated for GPP. The TP militants proposed that the FSLN should reorganize its activity around urban workers and the more proletarianized agricultural workers in cotton production. These militants proposed a return to Marxist orthodoxy, and the construction of a vanguard party within the working class. As a result of the conflict between the GPP strategy and the TP militants, the decision was made in October 1975 to expel the leaders of the TP. The members of the TP decided to accept their dismissal from the FSLN and to concentrate their militancy in factories and in the agricultural zones of the northwestern part of the country.[33]

A few months after these polemics, the internal crisis got worse with the combat death of one the original Sandinista cadres, Carlos Fonseca, in 1976. In addition, several other important leaders were captured, and others were exiled. During this period of crisis within the organization, a third current of opinion emerged called the Insurrectional Tendency (TI) or Third Current, which was led by the brothers Humberto and Daniel Ortega, together with Victor Tirado. They maintained that the conditions for an insurrectional civil war were already present in Nicaragua. They argued that society had undergone a rapid radicalization and that *Sandinismo* had to capitalize on this by forging agreements with the bourgeoisie. They were able to articulate an alliance with other opposition groups within the country to form a broad-based opposition movement. These efforts resulted in the formation of the "Group of Twelve" in October 1977. They also put into place an international solidarity and support network. The Group of Twelve entered into a series of agreements with representatives of all of the principal economic and political interests of the country (mostly represented in the UDEL). The archbishop of Managua, Miguel Obando y Bravo, facilitated these agreements.

The Church's involvement came from both the grassroots base community movement and within the hierarchy of the Church. Additionally many priests joined with the Sandinistas as individuals, including the prelate Gaspar García Laviana, Fr. Miguel D' Escoto, and the priests

---

[31] *Guerra Prolongada Popular*   [32] *Tendencia Proletariado*
[33] Nolan. *La ideología sandinista.*

Ernesto and Fernando Cardenal.[34] When the opposition journalist of the Conservative Party, Pedro Joaquín Chamorro (a member of one of the most important traditional families of Nicaragua) was assassinated in January 1978, the elites radicalized their positions with respect to the regime. At that moment almost all of Nicaraguan society openly challenged the Somoza government through a series of protests organized by students and workers.[35] The murder of one of the principal figures of the traditional elite class led all Nicaraguans to assume that anyone could be a victim of the dictatorship's repression. In mid-1978, the Broad Opposition Front (FAO)[36] was formed; it was composed of the Group of Twelve together with various labor unions, business associations, and diverse political groups. In turn the TP and GPP encouraged the creation of the Movement of the People United (MPU)[37] with more than twenty collectives of students, workers, peasants, and so on. The MPU functioned as the coordinator of the forces of the left, while the Group of Twelve and the FAO acted as links with the liberal democratic dissidents.

Armed activities intensified. The FSLN occupied the National Palace in August of 1978, taking numerous legislators as hostages. With this action they not only achieved the liberation of seventy prisoners, but they also collected a large amount of ransom money. This definitively marked the beginning of the insurrectional stage of the revolutionary process.

As direct confrontation against the dictatorship became more frequent at the end of 1978, the three tendencies initiated a process of reunification mediated by Fidel Castro. Finally in March 1979 unity was achieved with the formation of a Joint National Directive of nine members, three for each tendency. The unified leadership was composed of the Ortega brothers and Tirado for the TI; Bayardo Arce, Tomás Borge, and Henry Ruíz representing the GPP; and Wheelock, Luis Carrión, and Carlos Núñez of the TP. The Third Tendency was preeminent both in its strategic conception and in programmatic directives.[38]

In summary, the internal structure of the FSLN evolved throughout this military phase. The FSLN did acquire a centralized military hierarchy. As the movement grew (at the beginning of the 1960s) the administrative divisions within the FSLN corresponded to the territorial divisions of the country. There were Departmental and Zonal Directive Committees that

---

[34] Monroy García, Juan. *La Iglesia Católica en Nicaragua. Entre el poder y el compromiso con los pobres* (México D. F.: Universidad Autónoma del Estado de México, 2011).
[35] Tirado, *La Revolución Sandinista.*   [36] *Frente Amplio Opositor*
[37] *Movimiento Pueblo Unido*   [38] Nolan, *La ideología sandinista.*

reported directly to the National Directives (high political and military command). The base units were established through the militia – composed of guerrilla columns and commands – and through cells – rooted in the urban areas. All of these had a conspiratorial and clandestine character. The number of militants who actually belonged to the FSLN during its first fifteen years was very small; it did not surpass 150. Beginning in 1977 this number increased dramatically, and there was an open call to join in the mass insurrection.[39]

Mobilization Strategy during the First (Military) Phase (1959–1979)

The Sandinista leadership continually modified its mobilization strategy during the years of armed struggle. The FSLN adopted three distinct overall strategies that impacted whom they would seek to mobilize between 1961 and 1979: (1) foquismo (1961–1967), (2) the Maoist strategy of Prolonged Peoples' War (GPP) (1967–1974), and (3) the "insurrectional offensive" (1974–1979).

Foquismo was inspired in Nicaragua by the actions and triumph of the Cuban Revolution. It was built on the practice and the theoretical reflections of Che Guevara about that successful revolutionary movement.

Because the Cuban example was so compelling, the FSLN attempted to create one or two guerrilla groups in more remote and isolated parts of the Nicaraguan countryside. In those places they sought to mobilize and attain the support of the poor campesino population. This foquista military strategy resonated with the early twentieth-century experience of Sandino, when a mobilized campesino rebellion confronted the dictatorial government and opposed the presence of North American troops in the national territory. Foquismo was also compatible with the reality of the multitude of diverse armed movements that had emerged since the 1950s and sought to overthrow Somoza.

During this same period (1961–1967) the Sandinistas began to establish connections with other armed groups in the Caribbean Basin. In the mid-1960s some members of the FSLN made contact with the Rebel Armed Forces (FAR) of Guatemala, then led by Luís Turcios Lima. Because of this they slowly began to acquire some of the Guatemalans' tactics in their work with rural communities. These external contacts (including their experiences with Havana) contributed to their shift in strategy. When they suffered a serious defeat in August 1967, many

---

[39] Martí I Puig, *La izquierda revolucionaria en Centroamérica.*

important FSLN leaders died. This combined with the death of Che Guevara in Bolivia led to a reconsideration of foquismo. There was a clear need to recruit more and different kinds of militants, and so foquismo was eventually abandoned.

The "silent accumulation of forces" (also known as the Prolonged Peoples' War or GPP) became the official strategy after 1967. This strategy was adopted after careful consideration of the Chinese and Vietnamese experiences. The Sandinista leaders realized that they would have to clandestinely recruit a larger military force before actively engaging the Nicaraguan National Guard again. They also decided to seek the support of other social groups, in both rural and urban areas.[40]

Sandinismo, as the vanguard of the struggle against the Somoza regime, proposed that it should be engaged in preparing the people politically for a prolonged war by means of clandestine work among the masses.[41] This change in strategy was reaffirmed with the emergence of a new National Directorate together with the adoption of the "Sandinista Program of 1969." The FSLN deployed a program of political agitation among different marginalized urban groups, among progressive middle-class sectors, and in religious communities aligned with liberation theology. The Sandinistas were actively involved in organizing with the Association of Rural Workers (ATC),[42] the Revolutionary Student Front (FER),[43] the Secondary Students' Movement (MES),[44] the Association of Secondary Students,[45] and in the University Center of the National University (CUUN).[46] This activity within the student environment was especially important for recruiting and training Sandinista cadres and militants.

The political situation that emerged following the 1972 earthquake led to a slow political realignment within the diverse array of opposition groups. These realignments took place in a context characterized by growing social protest as well as increasingly violent repression. Although the dictatorship had attempted to impose a kind of complete domination over the traditional Conservative Party, other sectors within the dominant classes expressed their

[40] Marta Harnecker, *Los cristianos en la revolución sandinista (Entrevista a Luis Carrión)* (Buenos Aires: Ediciones Al Frente, 1987).
[41] Nolan, *La ideología sandinista.*   [42] *Asociación de Trabajadores del Campo*
[43] *Frente de Estudiantes Revolucionarios*   [44] *Movimiento Estudiantil de Secundaria*
[45] *Asociación de Estudiantes de Secundaria*
[46] *Centro Universitario de la Universidad Nacional*

dissatisfaction with the overt corruption of the Somoza family and their partners.[47]

The FSLN stormed and occupied the home of the minister of agriculture in December 1974. This action marked the start of a new phase of combat by the FSLN. This insurrectional strategy was fully operational in 1978 following the assassination of Chamorro and the triumph of the Third Tendency within the Sandinista leadership. As mentioned earlier, the conflict between the different tendencies arose because of the disagreements within the Sandinistas. The proponents of the Insurrectional Tendency insisted that the revolutionaries seek political agreements with the bourgeoisie while accelerating preparation for the final insurrection.

At the beginning of 1979, given the climate of intensifying repression and social protest, all of the political organizations in Nicaragua – both Conservative and Leftist – underwent a drastic realignment. The FAO fell apart because of conflicts within the leadership. The Ortega brothers then encouraged the construction of a new entity: the National Patriotic Front (FPN).[48] The FPN was composed of groups that had previously belonged to the MPU and the FAO. At the same time the Sandinistas began to mobilize almost all of the groups opposed to the dictatorship. Within a short time the insurrectionist strategy began to bear fruit.[49]

Finally, after the occupation of the National Palace in 1978, the FSLN orchestrated and coordinated the various armed fronts to advance a national offensive toward Managua from every major department of the country. When the final uprising began, the entire population was organized into Committees for Civil Defense (CDC).[50] And in the months prior to the fall of the regime, the CDCs were structured block by block to prepare the people for combat by developing an infrastructure that guaranteed water and first aid.[51]

Ideology during the First (Military) Phase (1959–1979)

In the beginning of the FSLN's history, its actions and ideology were nurtured from two major sources. Internally, the movement drew from

---

[47] Gilles Bataillon. *Génesis de las guerras intestinas de América Central (1960–1983)* (México D.F.: Fondo de Cultura Económica, 2008).

[48] *Frente Patriótico Nacional*

[49] Martí I Puig, *La izquierda revolucionaria en Centroamérica.*

[50] *Comités de Defensa Civil*

[51] Mónica Baltodano. *Memorias de la lucha sandinista* (Managua: Rosa Luxemburg Stiftung, 2010).

the century-long struggle in Nicaragua against the North American presence and the collusion between the US government and Nicaraguan dictators. In that sense the adoption of the term "Sandinista" provided the movement – early on – with an ideological identification and legitimation with strong historical resonance. The references to Sandino also called to mind the guerrilla leader who gathered around him an irregular army composed of campesinos who fought for land as well as freedom.

Two international events also influenced Nicaragua: the CIA-backed coup in Guatemala in 1954, which brought to bear many issues that were relevant in Nicaragua (agrarian reform, US military occupation, dictatorship with a high level of repression, etc.), and the triumph of the Cuban Revolution in 1959.

The Cuban Revolution had a strong influence on the revolutionary opposition in Nicaragua. The principal protagonists (Fidel Castro and Che Guevara) became ideological and material sponsors of guerrilla warfare.[52] They believed that the political actor would be the voluntary vanguard and the social actor would be the campesino.

When Carlos Fonseca and Tomás Borge were students at the National Autonomous University of Nicaragua (UNAN),[53] they were members of the Nicaraguan Socialist Party (PSN),[54] which at the time was the party aligned with Moscow. At the same time JPN was a political nucleus of an opposition movement within the university. Its members came from the PSN and the Conservative Party, and they experimented with the ideas coming from both Marxism and more nationalist ideologies. They also imagined themselves as the vanguard of a revolutionary foco. José Escobar, Julio Buitrago, and Silvio Mayorga were part of this group.[55]

Despite their convictions, foquismo was eventually abandoned for Prolonged Peoples' War (GPP). This strategic transition was accompanied by an ideological shift. Without abandoning the central postulates of Marxism, the Sandinistas distanced themselves from foquismo and began to adopt the proposals outlined by Mao Zedong in China and Ho Chi Minh in Vietnam. Nevertheless, this shift toward a Maoist strategy

---

[52] Fonseca, Carlos. *Bajo la bandera del sandinismo*. Managua: Editorial Nueva Nicaragua, 1982; Borge. *La paciente impaciencia*; Cabezas, Omar. *La Montaña es algo más que una inmensa estepa verde*. Managua: Editorial Nueva Nicaragua, 1982.
[53] *Universidad Nacional Autónoma de Nicaragua*   [54] *Partido Socialista Nicaragüense*
[55] Nolan, *La ideología sandinista*.

did not lead to a complete conversion to Maoist ideology. By this time the FSLN had constituted its own identity and nationalist ideology. In 1969 it proposed a uniquely Nicaraguan program to create a revolutionary government with the full participation of the whole population. This new ideology included the nationalization of the properties of Somoza and those that were in foreign hands, state control of foreign trade, agrarian reform, expansion of public education, the creation of new labor legislation, the integration of the Atlantic Coast into the nation, the emancipation of women, the creation of a "patriotic people's army," the end of "Yankee exploitation," and the establishment of solidarity ties "with all peoples who undertake the struggle for liberation."[56]

As the FSLN carried out its work within the student movement and in different rural communities, it began to be influenced by the ideas of liberation theology as new Catholic militants were integrated into their ranks. This generated another new source of ideas in the organization. The leaders of Christian Base Communities (CEBs) were integrated into the FSLN, as were student members of the Revolutionary Christian Movement (MCR).[57]

The strong debates (and subsequent internal ruptures) that took place between 1975 and 1977 led to a slow modification of the programmatic orientations of the FSLN. Sandinismo over time stepped further away from the classic postures of Marxism and more toward European social democracy. There were still important differences and debates that were rooted in twentieth-century Marxist revolutionary theory about the appropriate protagonists of the revolution (Wheelock argued that they were proletarians and Borge advocated for the campesinos). There were also conflicts within the Sandinista leadership about "the level of revolutionary consciousness of the people" and whether or not the conditions were ripe for an insurrection.[58] By the late 1970s, it was abundantly clear that the agreements promoted by the Insurrectionists (TI) – both with the civic political opposition groups opposed to Somoza and with different sectors of the bourgeoisie – clearly indicated abandonment of the ideals expressed in the 1969 program. From that moment the plans of a possible post-dictatorship government were built on the basis of three basic

[56] FSLN. *Programa del Frente Sandinista de Liberación Nacional* (Managua: DPEP-FSLN, 1969).

[57] *Movimiento Cristiano Revolucionario*. See Harnecker, *Los cristianos en la revolución sandinista*.

[58] Nolan. *La ideología sandinista*.

principles: political pluralism, mixed economy, and no international alignment.

The alliance between Sandinismo, sectors of the dominant class, and the mass movements made it possible for the final offensive of June-July 1979 to be successful. In July 1979, from Costa Rica, the formation of a provisional government was announced. Weakened in the face of a widespread national movement and the withdrawal of military and political support from the United States, as well as divisions within the National Guard and condemnation by the United Nations and the Organization of American States (OAS), the dictator Somoza fled Nicaragua on July 17, 1979. Two days later the guerrilla columns of the Sandinista Front entered Managua where they were received with enthusiasm by the people. After more than four decades of dictatorship, a new stage had begun.

THE SANDINISTAS IN POWER – THE SECOND PHASE (1979–1989)

Once the victory was consolidated in 1979, a broad group of economic and technical advisors, professionals, and social scientists collaborated with the Junta of the Government of National Reconstruction. During the period 1979–1980 the ruling Junta made all decisions by referencing "emergency powers." Following these directions, and through the Statute of the Republic of Nicaragua (August 1979), all existing and constitutional laws were abolished, and Congress, the Court of Justice, and the political remnants of Somozismo were dissolved.[59] In the words of Tomás Borge, the Sandinista government intended to create a "New Nicaragua" by abolishing all vestiges of the extinct dictatorship, the base of its economic power, and the external links that maintained it. The reconstruction of the national economy (which had been decimated by the war) was the primary goal. They proclaimed their intention to restructure society to reduce the inequalities of class, and to improve the standard of living of the poorest sectors of Nicaraguan society.[60] The plan was to carry this out by transforming the productive structure into a modern agro-industrial base from which to launch the exportation of coffee, sugar, meat, and bananas as principal products. These changes

---

[59] Thomas. W. Walker, *Nicaragua: The First Five Years* (New York: Praeger, 1985).

[60] John Booth, *The End and the Beginning: The Nicaraguan Revolution* (London: Westview Press, 1985).

began with the designation of a socialist agricultural enterprise called the "Area of the People's Property" (APP). The APP was established with confiscated property (about 20 percent of the arable land in the country). The Sandinistas used this property to launch a major program of agricultural investment, nationalization of foreign trade and banking, as well as the beginnings of a broad agrarian reform in 1981. But this re-distributive vision would require a new and stable government in order to be fully realized.

Formation and Consolidation of the New Revolutionary Government

The Junta undertook to establish anew the three branches of the new government: the Junta of Reconstruction, the State Council, and the Justice Department. The defense of the Revolution would be entrusted to a new national military force (replacing Somoza's National Guard) comprised and directed by ex-combatants of the FSLN. The Junta of Reconstruction instituted the "Program of the Government of National Reconstruction" – previously agreed upon in San José in July 1979. The program proposed a foreign policy of nonalignment, the creation of an effective democracy, and a system of social justice that would guarantee fully "the right of all Nicaraguans to political participation and universal suffrage," as well as the organization of functioning political parties that could compete without ideological discrimination (with the exception of parties and/or organizations that would seek a return to Somozismo).[61] The legislative power was to be constituted in the State Council that would be charged with sharing the functions of governance with the Junta. This State Council was supposed to ensure a broad representation of the social, economic, and political forces that were involved with the overthrow of the dictatorship. In December 1979, this initial agreement was broken by the FSLN,[62] and two of the members of the Government Junta (Alfonso Robelo and Violeta Barrios de Chamorro) resigned in protest in April and May 1980. This created early and serious friction between the more moderate middle-class sectors and the FSLN.

It is important to remember that the Government Program was initially drafted by the FSLN, and it was never truly accepted by the country's

---

[61] Naciones Unidas, "Programa de la Junta de Gobierno de Reconstrucción Nacional de Nicaragua" In *Nicaragua: El Impacto de la Mutación Política*, ed. United Nations, 105–120 (Santiago de Chile: Naciones Unidas, 1981).

[62] Increasing it to forty-seven members, thereby guaranteeing Sandinista predominance.

economic elites. The elite acquiescence to the program was achieved only under considerable pressure. The sole interest of the dominant classes was to overthrow the dictator. Similarly once the military victory was achieved, the concessions made by the Sandinistas to the elites were a tactical mechanism to ensure the cooperation of Western Europe and Latin America, Mexico and Venezuela. But to maintain this international support, it was necessary to respect the property rights of the elites and even to allow for their expansion.[63]

When the Junta of the Government of National Reconstruction issued its first decrees in July 1979, persons from different political tendencies were named as government ministers. This situation did not last long. In December 1979 the ministries were reconstituted in a way that allowed for greater control by the FSLN. Shortly before these events (November 1979), the Superior Council of Private Enterprise had declared its unwillingness to participate with the Government of National Reconstruction since, they claimed, there was no clarity about the scope and purpose of the APP; in other words, they believed that the private sector was being marginalized. Despite these disagreements, in February 1980 the People's Patriotic Block (BPP)[64] was formed. The BPP included an alliance between many diverse political parties, including the Independent Liberal party,[65] the People's Social Christian Party (PPSC),[66] the Communist Party, and the FSLN. Ultimately the only ones to stay in this union were the PPSC, the MPU, PSN, and the Sandinista Front. In June 1980 the remaining parties formed the Revolutionary Patriotic Front (FPR).

The heterogeneity of the coalition that participated in the overthrow of the dictatorship made the broad social transformation envisioned by the Sandinistas difficult from the outset. Within the coalition were diverse expectations for the Revolution. It turned out to be impossible to reconcile the alliance between the FSLN and the private sector (an indispensable part of the plan to rebuild the country).[67] The private sector conditioned its support for the Revolution on having significant economic and political participation within the government, which was never truly realized.

---

[63] Richard Harris, and Carlos Maria Vilas, *La Revolución en Nicaragua: Liberación Nacional, Democracia Popular y Transformación Económica* (México D.F.: Editorial Era, 1985).

[64] *Bloque Popular Patriótico*   [65] *Liberal Independiente*

[66] *Partido Popular Social Cristiano*

[67] José Luís Coraggio, and George Irvin, "Revolution and Pluralism in Nicaragua." In *Towards an Alternative for Central America and Caribbean*, ed. George Irvin and Xavier Gorostiaga, 285–286 (London: Unwin Hyman, 1985).

The Sandinistas' particular idea of pluralism implied that *they* would maintain control of the decisions that would advance the progressive political project. The so-called patriotic bourgeoisie[68] was asked to tolerate the idea (that the revolutionaries had proposed) of *popular hegemony* – in which the state would guarantee social distribution of economic surpluses without abolishing private property. Sandinismo was based on the idea of popular hegemony, but the private sector eventually came to reject it.

After a relatively short time, the FSLN began to see itself as the only true representative of the people, and to be dismissive of the idea of a broad consensus.[69] Regarding the criticisms made by the traditional Nicaraguan elites with respect to the Sandinista deviation from the original project of carrying out a democratic and pluralistic revolution, Sergio Ramírez (who was a member of the Government Junta) commented at the beginning of 1981:

The mixed economy and political pluralism belong to the very essence of the Sandinista design ... we have not departed from the original project. But if – due to the reality of a mixed economy – political pluralism and liberty of the press stop being compatible with the very survival of the revolution, we opt for the revolution to survive. The historical project of the Nicaraguan people is not circumstantial. The revolution did not win power through elections ... the scheme of our revolution belongs to the people. Everything could change in Nicaragua, except the hegemony of the people in the process.[70]

Participatory Democracy and Economic Development Strategies

During the early days of the Revolution, the new government was able to make profound political and socioeconomic transformations. At the same time the search for a new political model in which the participation of all social classes was permitted (a pluralistic model) *was* a sincere objective. Unlike other revolutionary movements there was never the expressed intention to establish a "dictatorship of the proletariat" or a single-party regime that would enforce state control over the means of production and abolish private property.[71]

---

[68] Generic name for the associations that accepted participation in the project of the new revolutionary government.

[69] José Luís Coraggio, and Rosa Maria Torres, *Transición y crisis en Nicaragua*, 116–117 (San José: Coordinadora Regional de Investigaciones Económica y Sociales, 1987).

[70] José Reveles, "El proceso, irreversible afirma Daniel Ortega," *Proceso*, July 18, 1981.

[71] José Luís Coraggio, *Nicaragua: Revolución y Democracia*, 79 (México D.F.: Coordinadora Regional de Investigación Económica y Social, 1985).

Nevertheless, six months following the triumph, significant changes in the ministries made it evident that the National Directorate of the Sandinista Front (and *not* the Junta of the Government of National Reconstruction) would control the key areas of power. Humberto Ortega, Henry Ruiz, and Jaime Wheelock were designated as ministers of defense, planning, and agriculture, respectively. Luis Carrión was named vice-minister of defense. As Tomás Borge (who was in charge of the Ministry of the Interior) affirmed in 1980, the FSLN controlled "the real instruments of power ... the revolutionary organizations, the party, the coercive bodies ... We could do what we wanted with the power that we had. We could remove the government and replace it with another if we had wanted."[72] In effect, the public slogan of political pluralism was interpreted through the Sandinistas' lens of popular hegemony. Because of this, popular organizations, the bourgeoisie, and even the capitalist class were forced to accept a subordinate position.[73] The contradictions of this project would lead to a permanent confrontation, thereby impeding the consolidation of the Revolution.

Similarly, relations between the Church and the Government of National Reconstruction also turned into a source of tension. CEBS participated actively in the revolutionary struggle. Following the triumph various progressive priests including Ernesto Cardenal, Fernando Cardenal, and Miguel D'Escoto, were appointed to positions within the government. In the opinion of the official Catholic hierarchy (and the Vatican), the presence of priests in the official state posts was an unequivocal sign that the Church was not maintaining its character as an impartial institution. The revolutionary leadership also articulated serious differences about the appropriate role of the Church. Periodic dialogues took place between the Catholic hierarchy and the priests who were more intimately linked with the Revolution, but in 1982 these communications were suspended because of a letter in which the bishops criticized the government.[74]

By 1982 the position of the Catholic Church was one of reproach. This posture even led some of the Church hierarchy to support the

---

[72] Jiri Valenta, and Esperanza Durán, *Conflict in Nicaragua: A Multidimensional Perspective* (Boston: Allen and Unwin, 1987).

[73] Richard Harris and Carlos Maria Vilas. *La Revolución en Nicaragua: Liberación Nacional, Democracia Popular y Transformación Económica* (México D.F.: Editorial Era, 1985).

[74] Michael Dodson, and Laura Nuzzi O'Shaughnessy, *Nicaragua's Other Revolution: Religious Faith and Politic Struggle* (Chapel Hill: The University of North Carolina Press, 1990).

counterrevolutionary struggle.[75] Although divisions among Nicaraguan clerics persisted, the Church eventually used its broad power to exert influence over the largely Catholic population to oppose the revolutionary project.

The Sandinistas were from the beginning cognizant of the constraints within which they had to work – such as dependence on the global capitalist market, probable confrontation with the United States, and human underdevelopment.[76] To overcome the first two limiting factors, the state appealed to its international allies. The Inter-American Development Bank and the World Bank were the principal sources of assistance during the first two years, but eventually the withdrawal of international support, the internal conflicts between the Sandinistas and the middle- and upper-class participants in the original coalition, and the war with the US-backed *Contras* (counterrevolutionaries) made the redistributive agenda difficult to maintain.

Another challenge for the Sandinistas was satisfying the economic demands of its own base – workers, peasants, artisans, small shopkeepers, professionals, and technicians – without alienating the people whose material interests were very different. The Sandinistas were forced to limit the programs with a populist orientation to maintain a political alliance of national unity, and they also had to balance the needs of the poor to avoid weakening the credibility of the Sandinista leadership with its base.[77] Their inability to do this eventually proved to be their downfall.

DEFEAT AND THE END OF A DREAM (1990)

After several years of a devastating civil war between the US-backed Contras and the Sandinista army, and under the weight of international pressure the government of Nicaragua committed to carrying out early presidential elections in February 1990, and to create the conditions for all of the representative political forces to participate in the process. Already in February 1989 coordination began through negotiations with the

---

[75] *Barricada*, Managua, June 6, 1986.
[76] Instituto de Estudios del Sandinismo, *Nicaragua, Cambios Estructurales y Políticas Económicas, 1979–1987* (Managua: Instituto de Estudios del Sandinismo, 1988).
[77] José Luís Coraggio. "Economía y Política en la transición: reflexiones sobre la revolución Sandinista." In *La Transición. Difícil: la Autodeterminación de los Pequeños Países Periféricos*, ed. José Luís Coraggio, Carmen Diana Deere, Orlando Núñez Soto, and Coordinadora Regional de Investigaciones Económicas y Sociales (México D.F: Siglo XXI Editores, 1986), 258.

business sector, represented by the Council for Private Enterprise (COSEP).[78] In negotiations with other regional leaders, Jaime Wheelock expressed willingness to end land confiscations. The government also indicated it would be willing to make periodic adjustments to the exchange rate to stimulate exports. Dialogue was initiated with opposition political parties, 1,900 ex-Somozista guards were pardoned, and the government made overtures to the Church by allowing the return of ten priests who had been expelled and by allowing Catholic Radio to broadcast again.[79] February 25, 1990, was set as the definitive date for carrying out these (early) presidential elections. The opposition parties had initially opposed moving up the date of the elections, but they eventually accepted and began to organize. When registration closed, in September 1989, ten parties had registered to take part in the competition: the Sandinista Liberation Front (FSLN); the Movement of Revolutionary Unity (MUR), both on the center-left. On the center-right: the Democratic Conservative Party of Nicaragua (PCDN), Central American Unionist Party (PUCA), National Unity Liberal Party, Social Conservatism and Social Christian; and on the right, the National Opposition Union (UNO). Of all these forces the Sandinista Front was the front-runner, both because it was the incumbent party and because it was the best organized. Being in power for a decade had allowed the FSLN to broaden its base. It had transformed from a political-military movement to a political party that had already triumphed in the elections of 1984. The benefits of leading the government were at the same time its Achilles' heel, since it was seen as responsible for the ongoing war and the difficult economic situation. With the slogan "we will win, everything will be better," the Sandinista Front and its candidates – for the presidency and vice-presidency, Daniel Ortega and Sergio Ramírez, respectively – expressed the willingness of the party to work for stabilization and national dialogue.

The UNO, on the other hand, was a coalition of diverse interests united in their desire to take political power away from the Sandinistas. The Program of National Salvation (promoted by this alliance) proposed policies to attract foreign investment and private initiative in the context of a market economy. It wanted to (1) eliminate the "dictatorial state method of planning, leading and controlling the economy"; (2) abolish

---

[78] *Consejo Superior de la Empresa Privada*

[79] Marta Casaus, and Rolando Castillo. *Centroamérica: Anuario 1990* (Madrid: Centro de Estudios de América Latina, 1991), 315–316.

obligatory military service; (3) enact constitutional reform; (4) reduce the size of the military and the defense budget; (5) carry out an integral agrarian reform "that would correct the abuses, limitations and deformations" that had been driven by the Sandinistas; and (6) promote a new labor code.[80]

The United States under President George H. W. Bush played an important role in supporting the electoral campaign of the National Opposition Union, through organizations such as National Endowment for Democracy (NED) and Freedom House. Between 1989 and 1990 the US Congress approved $12.5 million used to run the UNO campaign. The amount represented an average of $10 per voter, which would have been the equivalent of a foreign power investing $2 billion in the electoral process in the United States at that time.[81]

The Electoral Results and the Transition

In the elections held on February 25, 1990, Violeta Barrios de Chamorro (of UNO) was elected as the new chief executive, with 54.7 percent of the vote. Daniel Ortega of the FSLN received 40.8 percent. For the National Assembly, the Sandinistas received 42 percent of the popular vote (which gave them the right to 39 representatives), and the UNO received 53.9 percent of the vote, giving it 51 representatives. Eighty-five percent of the eligible population voted in the elections, the highest percentage of any election in Central America during that period. Numerous international observers proclaimed the election to be clean. The victory of the UNO was a major upset that caught the world by surprise. Every major pollster had predicted a Sandinista victory.

Several important factors explain the Sandinista defeat. With regard to economic policy, the Sandinistas defined the state as the principal engine of production, which led to a system of centralized planning that hindered the free functioning of the market. Politics and the uncritical acceptance of the FSLN leadership led to glaring inefficiencies in the state agro-industrial businesses, which were subsidized with credits despite their continuing lack of profitability. Also substantial investment in several large capital-intensive projects did not contribute in any way to economic growth. And

---

[80] Programa de Gobierno de la Unión Nacional Opositora (UNO). *Pensamiento Propio* 204 (1989): 67–74.

[81] William I. Robinson and Kent Norsworthy. "Elections and US Intervention in Nicaragua." *Latin American Perspectives* 85 (1985): 82–111.

the decision to invest hard currency in these projects made it more difficult for the state to address some of the most immediate needs of the population.

Moreover, the tendency to use these very fundamental economic considerations of how to structure the economy as a bargaining chip discouraged the financial sector from investing in the Revolution. The negotiations between the Sandinista government and the private sector (which were only restarted in 1988 after falling apart in the first two years of the Revolution) showed the belated desire of the revolutionary leadership to restore its former alliances from the years of national reconstruction. The incentives given to these private initiatives were made in a different economic climate (from the first year of the Revolution), and external resources were extremely limited. After almost a decade in power, the Sandinistas had lost the ability to bring people together. The concessions made to capitalism weakened their support from campesinos and workers. And they failed to convert those elite economic interests to their cause.[82]

During the previous decade the effects of the world and regional economic crises were augmented by the limitations of the economic structure inherited by Nicaragua, the armed conflict, and a commercial boycott promoted and maintained by the United States. For the revolutionary leadership their best argument in explaining the economic crisis was to remind its base about the impact of the US-backed boycott and the Contra war. There was also a strong tendency to idealize the socialist revolutions of the twentieth century, a weakness shared by other progressive movements around the world. The Left came to consider the loss of political liberty as a necessary condition of achieving social and economic equality.[83] After their electoral defeat, the Sandinistas recognized that they had reproduced some misguided practices common to other socialist countries. They had accepted the idea that there was only one kind of political party that could lead in the direction they wanted to go. This led to an excessive emphasis on control and the centralization of public management. Likewise, proclaiming themselves to be the revolutionary vanguard legitimated the implementation of the "government program."

---

[82] Carlos Maria Vilas. "Revolución, contrarrevolución, crisis: Nicaragua en la década de 1980." In *Centroamérica: Balance de una Década 1980–1990*, ed. Marta Casaus and Rolando Castillo (Madrid: Centro de Estudios de América Latina, 1992), 111–112.

[83] They promoted the idea that the private sector should limit its link with the revolution to the "productive area"; embracing the *logic of the majorities* was a slogan promoted by the revolutionary leadership.

The conflation of the party with the state undermined the credibility and the efficacy of the revolutionary project.

The collapse of the socialist system in Eastern Europe also contributed to the weakening of the Revolution. Revolutions in peripheral countries require broad international solidarity. The Nicaraguan Revolution counted on ample collaboration from the socialist world, until the political transformation in Eastern Europe changed the geopolitical context.

Carrying out the economic adjustments initiated in 1988, only two years before the elections, was also a problem for the Sandinistas. Initially the plan was to obtain financial help from abroad in order to achieve some real economic results before the election. The elections were moved up (due to strong international pressure), and they finally took place ten months earlier than expected.

The Sandinista Front did not consider the possibility that it could be defeated because it believed that the people would never vote against their own class interests. This triumphalist spirit allowed the Sandinistas to ignore the consequences of the growing loss of legitimacy of the revolutionary project. They seemed incapable of finding a way to end the civil war, and likewise they were unable to overcome the intense economic crisis that had undermined many of the gains that were achieved by the masses during the first years. Unemployment of almost 30 percent, the inefficiencies in both the public health and the educational systems, combined with extremely low salaries all contributed to diminishing the legitimacy of the regime.

Given this context the UNO's proposal of national salvation was quite attractive. It promised to improve incomes and to stabilize the economy – relying on the generous aid from North America – and it also promised to eliminate obligatory military service. The popular image of Violeta Barrios de Chamorro (widow of Pedro J. Chamorro, symbol of the anti-Somoza struggle) worked as a brilliant formula for the campaign of the opposition alliance. To a country exhausted by years of war, the conciliatory discourse that promised peace and bread, instead of war and hunger, turned out to be attractive to most voters.

CONCLUSIONS

Despite their failures, it is also clear that ten years was not sufficient time to overcome the vices inherited from decades of oppression, or to reestablish fully democratic institutions, especially while under attack by the United States. In Latin America, numerous examples demonstrate that only after a much longer period can the dead weight of cruel dictatorship be overcome. The Cuban Revolution also was not able to achieve significant results in its political economy until almost two decades after the initial triumph. On balance, the Sandinistas were able to achieve many important positive changes and victories. It is also important to take into account the adverse factors that impacted their achievements – specifically the war and the blockade imposed by the United States. Nevertheless, given the time that has elapsed, a recognition of the mistakes made by the Sandinista leadership during the 1980s is important to any kind of honest historical analysis.

Following the decade of Revolution, the traditional families – who possessed broad economic and political power – retook control of the state with a renewed and optimistic discourse. The context of neoliberalism and globalization allowed them to pursue a course of action that ran counter to the goals of social justice and economic equality that the Sandinistas had represented. Unlike the other Central American cases in this volume, there was no negotiated settlement in Nicaragua. Their commitment to an electoral democracy created a "winner take all" environment in 1989. Nevertheless, the FSLN remained as the largest political party in the country, and it has achieved several significant electoral victories in the intervening years.

Daniel Ortega, who still represents the Sandinista political party, is currently (2017) serving a third term as the president of Nicaragua. Although the party's democratic and socialist credentials may be questionable today, it has successfully survived the transition from armed revolutionary movement to political party.

Suggested Reading

Alegría, Claribel and Darwin Flakoll. *Death of Somoza*. Willimantic, CT. Curbstone Press, 1996.

Arias, Pilar. *Nicaragua. Revolución, relatos de combatientes del Frente Sandinista*. México. Siglo XXI Editores, 1981.

Borge, Tomás. *The Dawn Is No Longer Beyond Our Reach: The Prison Journals of Tomás Borge Remembering Carlos Fonseca*. Vancouver, BC: New Star Books, 1984.

Cardenal, Ernesto. *The Gospel in Solentiname*. Maryknoll, NY: Orbis Books, 2010.

Fonseca, Carlos. *Bajo la bandera del sandinismo*. Managua: Editorial Nueva Nicaragua, 1981.

Agudelo, Carlos, José Fajardo, and Gabriel García Márquez. *Los Sandinistas: Documentos, Reportajes de Gabriel García Márquez y otros*. 3ra edición. Bogotá: Editorial Oveja Negra, 1980.

Gott, Richard. *Rural Guerrillas in Latin America*. New York: Penguin Books, 1973.

Harnecker, Marta. *Nicaragua: el papel de la vanguardia: entrevista a Jaime Wheelock*. Buenos Aires: Editorial Contrapunto, 1986.

Henighan, Stephen. *Sandino's Nation: Ernesto Cardenal and Sergio Ramírez Writing Nicaragua, 1940–2012*. Montreal: McGill-Queen's University Press, 2014.

Kinzer, Stephen. *Blood of Brothers: Life and War in Nicaragua*. Cambridge, MA: Harvard University Press, 1991.

Palmer, Steven. "Carlos Fonseca and the Construction of Sandinismo in Nicaragua." *Latin American Research Review* 23 (1988): 91–109.

Ramírez, Sergio. *Adiós muchachos. A Memoir of the Sandinista Revolution*. Durham, NC: Duke University Press, 2011.

Sandino, Augusto Cesar and Sergio Ramírez. *El pensamiento vivo de Sandino*. Havana: Casa de las Américas, 1980.

Walker, Thomas W. *Nicaragua: The First Five Years*. New York: Preager, 1985.

Zimmerman, Matilde. *Sandinista: Carlos Fonseca and the Nicaraguan Revolution*. Durham, NC: Duke University Press, 2001.

Films

1979, año de la liberación (1979)
Alsino y el Cóndor (1982)
Bananeras (1982)
Carla's Song (1996)
El Inmortal (2005)
El sueño de una generación (2012)
La insurrección (1980)
La insurrección cultural (1980)
Nicaragua: A Nation's Right to Survive (1983)
Nicaragua: No Pasaran (1984)
Nicaragua Was Our Home (1985)
Nuestra reforma agraria (1982)
Palabras Mágicas (para romper un encantamiento) (2012)
Pictures from a Revolution (1991)
Sandino (1990)
Teotecacinte 83 (1983)
Under Fire (1983)
Walker (1987)
The World Is Watching (1988)

5

Armed Revolutionary Struggle in Colombia

The Colombian case is the most enduring and long-lived armed revolutionary struggle in the Caribbean Basin. The Revolutionary Armed Forces of Colombia (FARC),[1] The National Liberation Army (ELN),[2] and the April 19th Movement (M-19)[3] are the three most important guerrilla organizations of the twentieth century in Colombia.[4] Because of the longevity of the conflict, the Colombian case of armed revolutionary insurgency is somewhat unusual in the Latin American context. Unlike the other case studies discussed in this book, the Colombian history of insurgent violence is consistent throughout its modern history from the time of independence to the present. Eduardo Pizarro, one of the most eminent scholars of Colombian revolutionary movements has called Colombia a country with a "chronic insurgency."[5] The seeds for armed revolutionary struggle were sown in the early twentieth century, and the armed predecessors of the FARC insurgents were active by the beginning of the

---

[1] *Fuerzas Armadas Revolucionarias de Colombia*   [2] *Ejército de Liberación Nacional*
[3] *Movimiento 19 de Abril*
[4] There were three additional Cold War–era armed revolutionary organizations in Colombia: (1) The Popular Liberation Army (EPL – *Ejercito Popular de Liberación*), founded in 1967 as a Maoist alternative to the FARC and the ELN. It demobilized in 1991. (2) The Revolutionary Workers Party (PRT – *Partido Revolucionario de Trabajadores*) founded in 1982 as an offshoot of the Colombian Communist Party. It demobilized in 1992, and at that time there were 200 active guerrillas. (3) The Quintin Lame Armed Movement (MAQL – *Movimiento Armado Quintin Lame*) was an indigenous guerrilla group formed in 1984 to fight for indigenous lands. It demobilized in 1991 with approximately 130 fighters. These three groups were very small in comparison to the groups being discussed here.
[5] Eduardo Pizarro. "Elementos para una sociología de la guerrilla en Colombia." *Analisis Politico* 12 (Jan.–April 1991), Universidad Nacional de Colombia. Bogotá.

1950s. Moreover, during the 1980s and especially during the 1990s (after the end of the Cold War), two of the most important armed revolutionary groups, the FARC and the ELN, formed alliances with drug-trafficking cartels, which guaranteed their survival and expansion as military organizations for more than two decades after the collapse of the Soviet Union. So revolutionary armed struggle in Colombia predates the Cold War and continued into 2017.

According to many scholars, the guerrillas triumphed in Cuba and Nicaragua because of strong popular support and the ability of guerrilla movements to compromise the legitimacy of the state. In these two countries, as well as in Guatemala and El Salvador, dictatorships truncated all civic freedom through military repression. In Colombia, the relative (though precarious) stability of institutionality limited the possibilities for more radical alternatives. When compared to other countries of the region, Colombia has had a relatively stable democracy. It was also considered to be a "model country" in the fight against international communism because Colombia has always been reliably and unconditionally aligned with the interests of the United States. This position guaranteed long-term assistance for the Colombian government (from the United States) in the fight against armed revolutionary groups, and it came with some other material benefits, including more broad-based investment through the Alliance for Progress and more recently Plan Colombia.[6]

To understand why Colombia's political history follows such a distinct trajectory, it is necessary to examine the twentieth-century political history of the country.

THE COLOMBIAN STATE'S INTOLERANCE FOR SOCIAL PROTEST

Since the 1920s, the Colombian political and economic elites considered social mobilization to be a subversive and destabilizing practice. They feared that social protest movements in other countries could influence workers and campesinos in a context where the labor conditions were already very precarious. At the same time the Socialist Workers Party, the Revolutionary Socialist Party and the Communist Party emerged in

---

[6] In 1999, US President Bill Clinton and Colombian President Andrés Pastrana agreed on a new cooperative policy. "Plan Colombia" was originally intended to provide a comprehensive aid package for Colombia that would help the country resolve the Cold War conflict and would provide economic alternatives to coca production. By the time Plan Colombia was signed into law in 2000, it had become largely a military aid package that was designed to combat the threat of "narco-terrorism."

Colombia, and these political movements did not rule out violence. These radical political parties were explicitly tied to international communism after the Russian Revolution in 1917, and they were also engaged in both armed self-defense and limited offensive guerrilla actions by the late 1940s and 1950s.[7] The impact of this was to make the Colombian state firmly institutionalized around anti-communist ideology even before the beginning of the Cold War.

COLOMBIA'S HISTORICAL ALLIANCE WITH US INTERESTS

The Colombian government has always acted as an ally of the United States. Elite intolerance for any kind of social protest fit neatly with the interests of the United States in preventing "another Cuba." Many US officials falsely believed that the *Bogotazo* – the popular uprising in Bogotá in 1949 that erupted in response to the assassination of Jorge Eliécer Gaitán[8] – was a communist plot to disrupt the meeting of the Organization of American States. Many of the combatants in *La Violencia*,[9] a long and bloody civil conflict that dominated the 1950s, following on the heels of the Bogotazo, were then viewed with suspicion by officials (who were motivated by anti-communist fervor) in both the United States and Colombia. Colombia was also the only Latin American country to send troops to the Korean War, by which time the country was already the recipient of substantial military aid from the United States in the war against communism.[10] This preexisting cooperation between a broad segment of the Colombian elites and the United States in their opposition to communism had a significant impact in how armed revolutionary struggle played out in Colombia after the Cuban Revolution in 1959.

In 1958 a power-sharing agreement was implemented by the political elites of the Liberal and Conservative parties. The "National Front" (1958–1974) did put an official end to La Violencia, but the power of

---

[7] Torres Giraldo, Ignacio. *50 meses en Moscú* (Cali: Programa Editorial Universidad del Valle, 2005), 18.

[8] Gaitán was a populist political figure and charismatic Liberal party candidate for the presidency. His assassination sparked widespread popular violence and rioting.

[9] *La Violencia* in Colombia is the name given to a period of violent civil unrest that plagued the country for most of the 1950s. Half a million Colombians died in this conflict, which was nominally a power struggle between the Liberal and Conservative political parties in the country.

[10] Gary Leech, *The FARC: The Longest Insurgency* (London: Zed Books, 2011), 8–9.

the two dominant parties was consolidated and all other political groups were explicitly excluded. When there was a resurgence of campesino-based organizations commanded by communist leaders, the economic and political leaders of the country falsely alleged that this was part of an international communist plot inspired and supported by Cuba and China. Likewise, the Left read almost all government activity aimed at quelling violence and reestablishing control over territory as anti-communist reactionary violence.[11]

According to the National Center for Historical Memory, the armed conflict in Colombia can be understood as having passed through three distinct historical phases. The first phase (1958–1982) is marked by the early transition from a civil conflict between Liberal and Conservative factions into a guerrilla war between the state and forces that represented a broad swath of the Colombian Left. All three guerrilla organizations (FARC, M-19, and the ELN) were formed during this period. The second phase (1982–1996) was marked by territorial expansion and military growth of the guerrilla forces, and then a limited peace accord that ended the conflict with M-19. In addition this period marked the emergence of paramilitarism. Alliances were formed between ideologically diverse paramilitaries and the state, and there were also alliances between the FARC and the ELN and narco-traffickers. This escalation of violence resulted in a crisis and the partial collapse of the state. Toward the end of this phase was the resolution of the Cold War (1989) and a new Colombian constitution that was promulgated in 1991. The third phase (1996–2005) was marked by an exacerbation of the armed conflict due to the strength of the guerrillas as well as the growth and corruption of the paramilitaries. The actual periodization of the three organizations (FARC, ELN and M-19) under consideration varies slightly between the organizations.

THE REVOLUTIONARY ARMED FORCES OF COLOMBIA (FARC)

The FARC's origins were in campesino self-defense groups fostered by the Colombian Communist Party (PCC)[12] during the late 1940s. Between 1949 and 1964, the Communist Party developed a cyclical pattern of self-defense/guerrilla attacks in response to the escalating civil violence of *La*

---

[11] Grupo de Memoria Histórica, *Basta Ya! Colombia: Memorias de Guerra y Dignidad* (Bogotá: Imprenta Nacional, 2013), 117.

[12] *Partido Comunista Colombiano*

Violencia. In October 1949 the Central Committee of the PCC issued a communiqué in which it restated its commitment to grassroots militias dedicated to self-defense. This marked the beginning of armed revolutionary struggle in Colombia.

In 1953 Gustavo Rojas Pinilla launched a successful coup against the Conservative government of Laureano Gomez. The guerrillas and other self-defense groups[13] that were aligned with the communists agreed to demobilize after the coup (without handing over their weapons). They were subsequently subjected to political and social isolation. The already weakened Communist Party was now declared illegal by the dictatorship. In 1955 the military regime of Rojas Pinilla carried out a massive military offensive against a group of communist peasants located in the Municipality of Villarrica in the Department of Tolima. Armed actions quickly spread to neighboring regions. Approximately 5,000 government troops were dispatched to deal with a loosely organized resistance of approximately 800 campesinos, many of whom were not armed.

In 1958 Alberto Lleras Camargo, the first National Front president, implemented an amnesty law in an effort to pacify the country. Communist guerrillas decided (again) to abandon mobility (guerrilla warfare) and offensive violence in favor of armed colonization zones, a method that had already been tried and tested in the past by campesino self-defense organizations.[14] But in 1961 at the Ninth Congress of the PCC, they reversed their 1958 denunciation of violence and embraced the call for armed struggle again.[15]

Internal Structure during the First Phase (1958–1982) – FARC

The Colombian Communist Party had posited (in the context of the Cold War) that it was necessary to utilize all forms of struggle to take power. This thesis was adopted in 1961 and ratified at the plenary of the Central Committee meeting in June 1964. The FARC's birth is also associated with the Colombian army's attacks on the so-called independent republics of the south (in 1964 and 1966). Paradoxically it was these

---

[13] There were many groups of armed campesinos who had organized to defend their own communities during the years of civil conflict (La Violencia). They often aligned with the communist groups to achieve more effective security.

[14] Eduardo Pizarro, *Una democracia asediada. Balance y perspectivas del conflicto armado en Colombia* (Bogotá: Grupo Editorial Norma, 2004), 85–86.

[15] Gary Leech, *The FARC: The Longest Insurgency* (London: Zed Books, 2011), 13.

devastating government attacks against the communist guerrillas that made it possible for the FARC to obtain greater national and international visibility.[16]

The Revolutionary Armed Forces of Colombia, FARC, was officially founded in April 1966 and was the direct heir of the campesino resistance/self-defense movements of the 1950s. After 1966, overthrowing and taking control of the state became the central political goal. Leaders of these earlier campesino groups, Manuel Marulanda Vélez, Jacobo Arenas, Jaime Guaraca, and Efraín Guzmán, constituted the High Command of the FARC in 1966.

As was the case in the other countries in the Caribbean Basin, the birth and growth of the FARC was also tied to the Cold War politics of the era and the success of the Cuban Revolution in 1959. In its "Political Declaration of the Second Guerrilla Conference of the South Block" (1966), there was a reference made to the Tri-continental Conference in Havana and the "continuous aggressions of the U.S. imperialists against the peoples of Asia, Africa and Latin America." The FARC's political manifesto cited the Tri-continental's call for a "world-wide revolutionary movement for the peace and progress of all nations."[17]

The FARC's military structure was composed of a Secretariat with seven members, including the supreme commander (Manuel Marulanda). Immediately beneath this authority was the Central High Command, composed of approximately thirty guerrilla fighters, and below that seven "blocs," which were responsible for regional operations in different parts of the country. Within each bloc were fronts, columns, platoons, and squads. Marulanda was responsible for military decision making. Jaime Arenas was the intellectual/ideological leader of the FARC in these early years. Marulanda emphasized the importance of synthesizing military training and operations with political education and goals. He believed that guerrilla fighters had to be politically reflective at the same time as they were considering and reconsidering military strategy.[18] They were effectively adapting their structure throughout the 1960s and 1970s in response to changing conditions. During the second phase, they continued to evolve.

---

[16] Daniel Pecaut, *Las FARC. ¿Una guerrilla sin fin o sin fines?* (Bogotá: Editorial Norma, 2008), 42.
[17] Carlos Medina Gallego, "Las FARC-EP y el ELN. Una historia política comparada." Ph.D Dissertation (Universidad Nacional de Colombia, 2010), 108.
[18] Leech, The FARC, 16–17.

Internal Structure during the Second Phase (1982–1996) – FARC

In the early 1980s, the FARC was operating as the *de facto* government in its traditional rural strongholds in eastern Colombia and the south-central highlands. It had been establishing autonomous pockets of self-governance in these regions since the 1940s. As part of a change and expansion of its military strategy, it officially changed its name and internal structure at the Seventh Conference held in 1982. The name of the FARC was officially changed to Revolutionary Armed Forces of Colombia – People's Army, FARC-EP.[19] It also established clandestine "solidarity cells" to more consciously and effectively engage in political organizing work, in both rural and urban areas.

In November 1982 the president of Colombia, Belisario Betancur, issued a general amnesty to all guerrilla fighters in the hopes of initiating a peace process. The FARC signed onto the Uribe Accords in May 1984, setting the stage for a cease-fire and peace negotiations.[20] The FARC was not required to demilitarize, and it did not do so. While keeping its military structure intact, the FARC established a political party in 1985 with the assistance of the Communist Party to create a separate and more effective political arm. This new political party, the Patriotic Union (UP)[21] was immediately attractive to other Leftist forces in the country that had previously been excluded from political participation by the National Front arrangement.

Jaime Arenas (the political leader of the FARC) and Alfonso Cano (a young FARC commander from the Communist Party) headed the UP. With the birth of the UP, the clandestine solidarity cells were able to organize and operate openly and above ground. Arenas used the FARC military fronts to expand the influence of the political solidarity networks in undertaking an ambitious and legal organizing and education campaign among campesinos, urban intellectuals, students, and trade unions. Political representatives of every military front were asked to go from town to town to encourage sympathizers to organize "patriotic cells" or *juntas patrióticas*. These juntas were to be the local infrastructure of the new political party. By March 1986 there were at least 4,000 of these patriotic juntas. In the 1986 elections the UP elected 24 provincial deputies,[22] 275 municipal representatives, 4 senators, and 4 congressional

---

[19] *Fuerzas Armadas Revolucionarias de Colombia – Ejercito Popular*
[20] The Uribe Accords were signed in the Municipality of Uribe, which was the site of a corresponding cease-fire agreement.
[21] *Unión Patriótica*   [22] Comparable to state-level congressional representatives.

representatives and had a respectable showing by their presidential candidate, Jaime Pardo Leal. The military structure of the FARC remained intact while it undertook this political expansion.[23]

Because of the cease-fire mandated by the Uribe accords, both the FARC and the Colombian military were prohibited from engaging in official military actions. Anti-communist elements within the Colombian military and the political elites organized new paramilitary groups – many of which were composed of "off-duty" military personnel – to attack guerrillas, as well to engage in systematic repression of the political leadership and membership of the UP.

In 1986 President Virgilio Barco came to power. Also by this time there was substantial opposition within the Colombian political hierarchy to the peace process, which was formally ended in 1987 along with the cease-fire. After this point the military and paramilitary forces of the state used disappearances, massacres, and attacks to eliminate the leadership of the UP. Targeted assassinations of the entire leadership and base membership of the UP escalated. By 1990 more than 2,000 UP members had been assassinated, including two presidential candidates (Jaime Pardo Leal and Bernardo Jaramillo) and 4 elected congressmen. Jaime Arenas also died (of cancer) in 1990, marking the end of this political project of the FARC.[24] In essence, the party was exterminated. After this assault on the most viable democratic alternative for the Left, all hope for a peaceful resolution to the conflict with the FARC ended.

Internal Structure during the Third Phase (1996–2005) – FARC

The annihilation of the UP was also the annihilation of the political leadership of the FARC. After the mid-1990s the FARC had become a more reactionary military organization that had survived the end of the Cold War through an alliance with international drug traffickers. This is not to say that the FARC had no political agenda, but it had no real political leadership. Moreover, the consolidation of "hard-liners" within the military and political leadership of the national government made a political solution virtually impossible. Despite the fact that formal negotiations continued during the late 1990s and early 2000s, the civil conflict became increasingly militarized between 1996 and 2005.

The military structure of the FARC remained intact, and it was able to significantly expand its military operations, as well as terrorist actions

---

[23] Leech, *The FARC*, 25–29. [24] Ibid., 29–32.

(kidnappings, assassinations, etc.) along with its reliance on narcotics trafficking. Throughout the entire history of the FARC, the question of "who" should be recruited to the FARC evolved but maintained some consistent elements as well.

Mobilization Strategy during the First Phase (1965–1982) – FARC

After its formal creation in 1966, the FARC did not immediately develop a true military capacity; consequently, it quickly became vulnerable. This led to several significant military defeats. During this period, the main substantive goal of the movement was meaningful agrarian reform, a goal that defined its mobilization strategy to a large extent. That is, the FARC recruited campesinos who were initially mobilized for self-defense and the preservation of some autonomy in the face of government repression. The FARC appealed to these campesinos with promises of autonomy and land.

Mobilization Strategy during the Second Phase (1982–1996) – FARC

During the second phase of expansion (in the 1980s), the guerrilla movements in Colombia reached their zenith. In the late 1980s, the FARC instigated its alliance with drug traffickers as the socialist world began to collapse. This alliance with the highly profitable drug cartels gave the FARC capital to invest in military strength. At the same time, the guerrilla group declared that it was time for a "revolutionary situation" because the protest of the masses had adopted an "insurrectionary character." Consequently, it decided to double its fronts, expanding from twenty-four to forty-eight, and taking territory where it had no previous presence. The goal was to take power within eight years.[25] During this period, kidnapping and extortion practices were used to obtain resources for the struggle because (unlike the ELN) the FARC never received logistical or financial support from the Soviet bloc. As the resources of the FARC grew and its profile became more prominent, the mobilization abilities of the organization snowballed. While still recruiting a primarily campesino base, it was able to expand its mobilization efforts into many parts of the country where it had not previously been present.

[25] Pecaut, *Las FARC*, 49.

Mobilization Strategy during the Third Phase (1996–2005) – FARC

In the late 1990s, in the context of the ongoing peace talks between the FARC and the Pastrana government, the Colombian government withdrew its military forces from a 16,200-square-mile "clearance zone" (*Caguán*), effectively turning it over to the FARC. This territorial autonomy, combined with the increased financial incentives of the illicit narcotics industry allowed the FARC to strengthen its military capacity to unprecedented levels. At the same time that the ideological foundations of the Cold War were disintegrating and the political legitimacy of the FARC was eroding, the FARC found itself in a position of unprecedented strength. While maintaining – at least nominally – its commitment to social justice and Marxism-Leninism, the FARC was actually able to leverage the poor economic situation (and joblessness) caused by neoliberal reforms to recruit new members, still mostly among the campesino base.

In 2002, Álvaro Uribe was elected on a hard-line platform of confronting the FARC and ending Pastrana's peace process. Colombians – weary of the ongoing conflict and the seeming futility of negotiating with FARC while its military capacity only grew – elected Uribe, with the resolve to return to a military strategy of ending the conflict. The return to open conflict gradually diminished the FARC's mobilization capacity, as it became increasingly discredited in the public eye. The mobilization strategies of the FARC were in some measure always determined by ideology, but ideology also emerged in some organic ways from the structures and strategies of the organization.

Ideology during the First Phase (1964–1982) – FARC

During the years 1964 to 1981, the FARC was politically dependent upon the Communist Party, and all of its activity was channeled through party. Although the party had already adopted (in 1961) the thesis of the "all forms of struggle," it considered the self-defense and guerrillas forces under its political influence to be primarily defensive instruments that served as a strategic reserve in the process of accession to power. As a result, not even during the worst moments of official repression did the leadership of the party move to the countryside. The party followed the Soviet guidelines of "peaceful coexistence" and "*détente*," which openly opposed the Cuban model of guerrilla warfare.[26] Nevertheless

---

[26] The Tri-continental was a defining moment between Cuba and the USSR for Latin American communist parties, when many chose to stand in good terms with both.

the guerrillas and paramilitaries under the guidance of the party during these early years had their origins in agrarian struggles that had been born prior to the Cuban Revolution, and their claims were more closely linked to the needs of campesinos (land reform) than to domestic or international revolutionary motivations. The agrarian conflicts of the first half of the twentieth century gave birth to campesino movements (like the self-defense groups) that stemmed from processes of colonization and resistance. This eventually gave rise to the mobile columns of the guerrillas and the birth of the FARC-EP. In other words, the guerrillas were just one variable in the combination of "all forms of struggle." While it cannot be said that the Communist Party created the FARC, its strong Marxist-Leninist ideological influence and political leadership were undeniably crucial.[27]

Ideology during the Second and Third Phases (1982–2005) – FARC

The creation of the Patriotic Union (UP) marked a different period for the ideology of the FARC. While it continued to pursue a rural military strategy, it was also building urban and semi-urban political cells to form the basis of the new political party. The more moderate and politically oriented leadership of the FARC devoted itself to the creation and promotion of "solidarity cells," which would form the basis of the UP. When the UP was eliminated through violent repression by the Colombian military, the political arm and the more ideologically sophisticated segment of the FARC was eliminated as well. What was left by the late 1990s was a more militant and dogmatic military organization that was less capable of engaging in negotiations.

After the Cold War ended and the M-19 was demobilized, the FARC would nominally maintain a commitment to Marxism-Leninism for almost a decade. After the pink tide swept the region in the early 2000s, and especially after the election of Uribe in 2002, the FARC adopted a more Pan-American "Bolivarian" discourse and sought alliances with other Colombian armed movements as well as sympathetic Leftist governments in the region.[28] The ideology of the FARC, while never entirely

---

[27] Luís Fernando Trejos, "Aproximaciones a la Actividad internacional de una organización insurgente colombiana. El Ejército Popular de Liberación (EPL). De China a Cuba vía Albania." *Revista Investigación y Desarrollo* 21 (2012): 371–394.

[28] Hugo Chavez forged what he called a "Bolivarian Revolution" when he came to power in Venezuela in 1998. Chavez's reference to Simon Bolivar's Pan-American project helped him broaden the appeal of his nationalist socialist project to the rest of the continent. The appeal to a Bolivarian spirit behind his anti-imperialist (anti-US) project provided an

abandoning its original principle of social justice and redistribution, became increasingly difficult to reconcile with its growing criminal activities.

THE NATIONAL LIBERATION ARMY (ELN)

The occupation of the town of Simacota in the Department of Santander on January 7, 1965, marked the birth of the National Liberation Army (ELN).[29] Camilo Torres Restrepo, a Roman Catholic priest and a leading Marxist intellectual, joined with the ELN during its earliest days. Camilo Torres was an important figure in the liberation theology movement, and the development of this religious movement impacted the evolving ideology of the ELN. Torres was killed in combat on February 15, 1966, in Patio Bonito Santander.[30] After his death the leadership included several other Roman Catholic priests, including the Commander Manuel Pérez (known as the "Cura Pérez"), and they continued to be heavily influenced by liberation theology.

Internal Structure during First Phase (1965–1983) – ELN

The internal structure of the ELN during the 1960s was based on Che Guevara's foco theory. The ELN, under the leadership of Fabio Vásquez Castaño, had emerged from the Revolutionary Liberal Movement (MRL)[31] – a radical outgrowth (but an electorally based political party) of the Liberal Party. The MRL held its first convention in March 1960. Vásquez Castaño was among a group of young MRL members who went to Cuba in the early 1960s and subsequently decided to pursue armed struggle.

Because they were able to capitalize on the existing structure of the MRL, the ELN counted on a fairly well-established network and infrastructure from the beginning. Because of his popularity and national profile, Camilo Torres's death and martyrdom in February 1966 led many radical Liberals and dissidents to join the ELN, and Vásquez Castaño was able to expand the military presence of the ELN throughout

---

opportunity for the FARC to ally itself with "tide" of Leftist governments that were in power in the region during the first decade of the 2000s.

[29] Vargas, Alejo. *Guerra o solución negociada. ELN: origen, evolución y proceso de paz* (Bogotá: Intermedio Editores, 2006), 121.

[30] For a classical and complete work on Camilo Torres, see Broderick, Walter, *Camilo el cura guerrillero* (Bogotá: El Ícono Editorial, 2013).

[31] *Movimiento Revolucionario Liberal*

1966. At the end of that year, there were two major columns of the ELN, the larger of which was composed of at least forty guerrilla fighters. As the size of ELN's army expanded in the late 1960s, so did its vulnerability to military assault. As a result, the largest detachments (including Vásquez Castaño's) were divided into smaller guerrilla focos in 1967 and 1968.

During the rest of the 1960s, internal divisions and power struggles beset the ELN. Consequently it entered into cooperative negotiations with the FARC and also expanded urban recruitment.[32] The ELN's Central Command (COCE) has always represented the highest level of authority within the organization. Underneath the COCE is a National Directorate, which had approximately twenty-three members. This National Directorate served as an intermediary body between the military fronts of the organization and the COCE.

The 1970s was a period of crisis for the ELN. It suffered several debilitating military defeats, and the deaths of several important leaders. In 1973 a major military offensive by the Colombian Army left 135 of ELN's 200 active combatants dead. Soon after this, the first National Assembly was held in July 1974 in the Department of Antioquia. During this meeting the ELN was forced to establish several new fronts as its existing military fronts had been decimated.[33]

Vásquez Castaño, who was relentlessly pursued by the Colombian armed forces, left for exile in Cuba in August 1974; this eventually resulted in a change of leadership within the ELN. El Cura Pérez and Nicolás Rodríguez Bautista (alias Gabino) officially took over the leadership. By the mid-1970s they had begun to restructure and shift their focus to political organizing work, which had been ignored during the first decade. Once the internal crisis was overcome by the early 1980s, a new National Directorate was formed in October 1983 by the three fronts that remained at the time: the Domingo Laín Sáenz Front, the Camilo Torres Restrepo Front, and the José Antonio Galán Front. This marked the beginning of the second phase for the ELN.

Internal Structure during Second Phase (1983–1996) – ELN

The ELN from 1983 to 1986 almost quadrupled in size. This growth was the result of the broader popular struggle in Colombia. At the same time

---

[32] René de la Pedraja, *Wars of Latin America, 1948–1982* (Jefferson, NC: McFarland, 2013).
[33] Medina Gallego, ELN, 151–152.

the oil and gold economies combined with the adoption of illegal tactics (e.g., kidnapping and extortion) meant that the ELN had access to economic resources that also facilitated its growth.

It expanded its geographic presence across a broad swath of the country and maintained a federalist system of "consensual democracy."[34] The Central Command structure of the ELN was required to consult with the National Directorate and the guerrilla fronts. This more democratic structure has long complicated its ability to negotiate with the Colombian government because it is required to achieve a consensus before signing any agreements.

Internal Structure during the Third Phase (1996–2005) – ELN

The ELN continued to expand its military base through the end of the 1990s and into 2000. Unlike the FARC, it was not directly involved in drug trafficking until 1998; rather, it focused on kidnapping and extorting employees of multinational oil companies. After 1998 it also began taxing coca and marijuana farmers, particularly in the province of Bolivar where they maintained their base of operations.

The beginning of the new century marked the beginning of the decline of the ELN. Because of its model of small, dispersed armed foci, it was particularly vulnerable to paramilitary attacks that resulted in considerable losses of both personnel and territory in the early 2000s. Although the ELN briefly engaged in peace talks in 2001, 2002, 2004, and 2005, the Colombian government did not seriously engage the ELN in any negotiations after 2000. Although the group continued to survive, it suffered from internal divisions. Since the agreement between the FARC was ratified in December 2016, negotiations between the ELN and the Colombian government have been reignited. The resolution of the conflict with the FARC has provided strong new incentives for both parties to resolve the conflict with a formal agreement.

Mobilization Strategy during the First Phase (1965–1980) – ELN

Fabio Vásquez had finished his education and received his military training (along with the rest of the original foco of the ELN) in Cuba, and so the

---

[34] León Valencia. "The ELN's Halting Moves toward Peace." In *Colombia: Building Peace in a Time of War*, ed. Virginia M. Bouvier (Washington, DC: US Institute of Peace Press, 2009), 102.

Cuban model initially influenced him when he was defining the mobilization strategy of the ELN.[35] The triumph of the Cuban Revolution led to the widespread belief in the region that it was possible to replicate this experience with only a small rural-based guerrilla foco, and without the help of political organizations. This idealism and the concurrent belief in the possibility of quick victory by revolutionary militants with little to no training was appealing to students and more urban elements of the social movement in Colombia. Although this had a big impact on who was originally mobilized into the ELN, it also led to a series of disastrous military losses. Jacobo Arenas stated that the groups formed in the early sixties

did not assimilate the whole [Cuban] experience, nor did they care to understand the combination of circumstances and events that made possible the victory of socialism on the island; it was believed, in good faith, that the rebellion of an armed group alone could make the revolution occur and its triumph inevitable and immediate ... This led to the belief that *only* [emphasis added] the guerrilla organizations in the mountains or the tactical combat units in the cities were important.[36]

Initially the organization was also influenced by the recruitment and martyrdom of Camilo Torres, and so much of the early recruiting was done within the context of the Catholic Church and the growing popularity of liberation theology.

The student movement (the National University Federation – FUN),[37] particularly in the Industrial University of Santander, also played an important role in the formation of the ELN in 1965. In addition there were three important revolutionary youth organizations that had been formed in Colombia, largely in response to the Cuban Revolution – the Students and Workers' Movement of Colombia (MOEC),[38] the Union of Communist Youth of Colombia (UJCC),[39] and the Liberal Revolutionary Youth Movement (JMRL).[40] Some members of the university student organizations as well as individuals from the MOEC and JMRL joined the emergent ELN. Inspired by the idea of a socialist revolution, youth groups in those years tended to be more closely associated with the ELN,

[35] Luís Fernándo Trejos. "Un actor no estatal en el escenario internacional. El caso de las FARC-EP (1964–2010)." PhD Dissertation, Instituto de Estudios Avanzados de la Universidad Santiago de Chile, 2013.

[36] Quoted in Medina Gallego, "Las FARC-EP y el ELN," 176.

[37] *Federación Universitaria Nacional*   [38] *Movimiento Obrero Estudiantil Campesino*

[39] *Unión de Juventudes Comunistas de Colombia*

[40] *Juventudes del Movimiento Revolucionario Liberal*

and indeed they played an important role in its formation. In addition to the student groups, radicalized sectors of some trade unions, especially in the oil industry, also allied themselves with the ELN.[41]

In October 1973 the organization was almost entirely wiped out in a crushing military defeat near the Anorí River in Antioquia. Vásquez went into exile in Cuba and was eventually expelled from the organization. From the mid-1970s to the early 1980s, the ELN's strategy revolved around rebuilding its resources and its military capacity. It did this primarily through targeted kidnappings and extortion, targeting wealthy landowners and politicians. Its mobilization was consequently more oriented toward campesinos and the rural base. Campesino fighters came to the struggle with a higher degree of military preparation and knowledge of the terrain than had the students and urban workers from the earlier period.

Mobilization Strategy during the Second and Third Phases (1980–2005) – ELN

During the 1980s and early 1990s, the ELN expanded its geographic presence in twenty-three departments across Colombia. It maintained a strategy of supporting small armed nuclei in remote areas with the goal of maintaining relationships within the communities in which it operated. To do this the ELN guerrillas engaged in various social activities in these communities. This model helped overall mobilization efforts but made them more vulnerable to military attack. This combined with its more democratic decision-making structure, as well as its rivalry with the much larger FARC hindered its ability to negotiate an end to hostilities with the government.

Both the military activity of the ELN along with the mobilization strategy consistently had an overwhelming impact on the evolution of the organization's ideology. There are many ideological similarities between the ELN and the other Cold War Colombian armed groups, but there are also some significant differences.

Ideology during the First Phase (1965–1980) – ELN

Originally the ELN followed a nationalist and anti-imperialist ideology, distant from Marxist discourse and inspired by the idea of "national

---

[41] Vargas, *Guerra o solución negociada*, 152–153.

liberation." Early documents of the ELN evidence the influence of the thesis of "democratic revolution," which was characteristic of the Liberal Revolutionary Movement (MRL).[42] The ELN's discourse proposed a struggle inspired by the ideas Jorge Eliécer Gaitán, calling for both "Liberals and Conservatives to overthrow the oligarchies of the two parties."[43] The role of the Catholic Church in the early ideology of the ELN was also extremely important.

Starting in the 1950s, the Catholic Church began a process of radical transformation. The Vatican began to promote a program to make the Church more relevant to Catholics around the world, especially in Latin America, which was home to the largest segment of Catholics anywhere. This program, called Catholic Action, sent hundreds of European priests to Latin America, as well sending a large contingent of young Latin American priests to Europe for their education. Many in this new generation of young priests were trained in the social sciences as well as in theology. These efforts culminated in the Second Vatican Council (Vatican II). Vatican II, the most recent ecumenical council in the history of the Catholic Church, opened in October 1962 and closed in December 1965. The council resulted in significant changes in the life of the Church and the everyday lives of Roman Catholics.

One of the central problems for Latin American Catholicism was a shortage of priests, especially in poor urban and rural areas. After Vatican II and its emphasis on making the Church more accessible to laypeople, many large parishes in Latin America trained lay ministers (catechists) to lead smaller Christian Base Communities (CEBs).[44] One of the primary activities of these CEBs was literacy training and Bible study. The poor people who were engaged in reading the Bible were often radicalized. This, combined with the radicalization of many priests (such as Camilo Torres and Manuel Pérez) gave birth to a new way of being Catholic and a new kind of theology that involved looking at the Bible and the Church through the lens of the poor. This movement had a strong influence on the ELN's ideological evolution during this early period.

The overwhelming defeat of the "Anorí" operation in 1973 unleashed a crisis that had already been brewing due to the personalistic and caudillo-style leadership of Fabio Vásquez Castaño. It was not only the military and political weakening of the most important ELN front that led to this crisis, but also the ideological disdain toward the idea of

[42] *Movimiento Revolucionario Liberal*   [43] Vargas, *Guerra o solución negociada,* 230.
[44] *Comunidades Eclesiales de Base*

a revolutionary organization with a strong popular base. Military actions were favored over politics, and executions were used to deal with internal political differences (rather than using dialogue and other democratic measures). Many members of the ELN were disenchanted by foco theory and Guevarista purity, as well as the caudillo-style leadership of Vásquez Castaño[45].

After Vásquez Castaño left the country in 1974, the ELN leadership began to question the validity of the armed struggle, a new perspective that came to be called the *replantamiento* or "rethinking." The purpose of this new process was to determine whether or not to continue to relegate the political work with the country's grassroots movements to a lower priority. There was a strong sense that the lack of political organizing work would keep the ELN marginalized. Other factors also led to adjustments to the ideology of the ELN. The military defeats at the hands of the Colombian army and the collapse of the ELN's "urban network" in 1972 played important roles in the rethinking, as did the achievements of guerrillas in the southern cone (i.e., the Tupamaros in Uruguay, and the Montoneros and the ERP-PRT in Argentina) who had managed to make strong connections with the working classes and popular masses in their countries. A final determining factor was the assimilation into the ELN of new social leaders from urban areas who identified the need for community and political work among the masses.[46]

Ideology during the Second and Third Phases (1980–2005) – ELN

The ELN did not radically alter its ideology after 1980. It continued to follow an ideology based on a Marxist concept of social justice with a commitment to pursue both a military strategy and political work simultaneously. Its ability to engage effectively in peace negotiations was hampered by its geographical dispersion as well as its less centralized decision-making authority. Despite this, tension existed within the ideological leadership of the ELN between those who promoted more armed confrontation and those who desired a negotiated peace.

The end of the Cold War and the increased reliance on criminal activities (kidnapping and extortion and – after 1998 – drug trafficking) compromised the ideological commitment of the ELN. Still, like the FARC, it has remained an inherently political organization with a stated commitment to social justice and economic equality throughout its history.

---

[45] Vargas, *Guerra o solución negociada*, 231–233.   [46] Ibid., 235–237.

THE APRIL 19TH MOVEMENT (M-19)

The April 19th Movement (M-19)[47] was formed in the context of a wave of broadly populist movements throughout Latin America. The young Colombian militants of the National Popular Alliance (ANAPO) – a nationalist and populist party led by General Gustavo Rojas Pinilla – were influenced by political trends in South America, including the return of Peronism in Argentina and Salvador Allende's election in Chile.[48] Rojas Pinilla ran for president in 1970, and lost in what was considered by many to be a fraudulent election (stolen by the National Front).

Starting in 1966 Jaime Bateman Cayón led the formation of the first urban network of the FARC before he and his group were expelled in 1970. For a few years after this Bateman continued to pursue the goal of organizing an urban guerrilla army through a project called *Los Comuneros*. After the rise in popular discontent over perceived electoral fraud in 1970, various sectors of ANAPO formed an armed unit. Later, in 1973, and as a result of the confluence of interests between *Los Comuneros* and the so-called Anapista armed nuclei, the M-19 was officially created. Some of the movement's principal founders (in addition to Bateman) were Carlos Toledo Plata, Álvaro Fayad, Iván Marino Ospina, and Andrés Almarales. Important leaders such as Carlos Pizarro, Vera Grave, and Antonio Navarro Wolff later joined them.

The M-19 was a comparatively short-lived guerrilla group whose history crosses between the first and second phases of the larger history of armed revolutionary violence in Colombia. From its inception in 1972 to the resolution of peace negotiations in 1990, it represented a less ideologically dogmatic (and more moderate) way of advocating for social democracy.

Internal Structure during the First Phase (1970–1980) – M-19

M-19 was officially founded in 1973 when the armed militant sector of ANAPO (led by Andrés Almarales) allied itself with Bateman's urban

---

[47] *Movimiento 19 de Abril*

[48] ANAPO was a political party formed by then ex-president Gustavo Rojas Pinilla in 1960. The party had an anti-communist but still populist ideology. Rojas Pinilla ran for president in 1970, and when he lost to the Conservative National Front candidate Misael Pastrana, many Colombians believed the results to be corrupted. The resulting social mobilization (to protest the election results) prompted Pastrana's government to declare a state of siege. When M-19 emerged publicly in 1974, it explicitly connected its claims to the election of 1970.

comuneros. Three other Anapista congressmen joined with Almarales and Bateman to form the M-19. The new guerrilla organization had a political wing (which built upon the existing political organization of ANAPO) and a military wing. It established a military command structure, at the same time maintaining its (primarily urban) grassroots political organizing activity under the cover of ANAPO.[49] It called itself the April 19th Movement, referencing the 1970 election that was held on that day. Its first public act was the dramatic theft and appropriation of Simón Bolívar's sword from the *Quinta de Bolívar Museum* in Bogotá on January 17, 1974.

The question (for both ANAPO and the M-19) after 1974 was whether or not to maintain the alliance between the political party and the armed movement. The alliance was tentatively maintained for a few years, but by the middle of 1975 (after the death of Rojas Pinilla), the two organizations had officially parted ways. ANAPO was dissolved soon after this.

Because of the urban nature of the majority of M-19's recruits, Bateman pursued an urban strategy. This eventually created a conflict between urban labor leaders and the intellectual leadership of the M-19. José Raquel Mercado, the president of the Colombian Workers' Confederation (CTC)[50] was kidnapped and assassinated by the M-19 in 1976, after being accused of corruption. This caused a rift within the M-19 membership. Bateman conducted a survey of the membership, and the results were the basis for ongoing debates within the organization. The organization adjusted its ideology and strategy in response to the wishes of the base, but it was still unable to establish itself as a viable revolutionary alternative during this early period.

Internal Structure during the Second Phase (1980–1996) – M-19

When the Sandinistas marched triumphantly into Managua in July 1979, the M-19 returned from the brink of dissolution. The urban insurrectionary nature of the Sandinista victory created a renewed sense of optimism around the possibilities for the M-19. It was able to promulgate the excitement around the Sandinista victory into enthusiasm for recruitment, and their numbers grew.

---

[49] Ana Carrigan's journalistic account of the meeting between Almarales and Bateman in a café in 1972 is a lively story of the formation of the M-19. See Ana Carrigan, *The Palace of Justice: A Colombian Tragedy* (New York: 4 Walls, 8 Windows, 1993), 77–79.

[50] *Confederación de Trabajadores Colombianos*

In February 1980 the M-19 seized control of the embassy of the Dominican Republic and took several prominent diplomatic officials hostage, including the US ambassador. Bateman demanded both money and the release of several M-19 leaders who were in prison. The standoff lasted until April 27 when the Colombian government allowed the occupying guerrilla unit safe passage to Cuba. The hostages had privately (and secretly) raised $1 million, which was given over to the M-19. Bateman used these resources to launch two small invasions (from Panama) on the Pacific coast of Colombia. Both invasions were eventually unsuccessful. Bateman attempted another sea-invasion in 1981 after purchasing an old German steamer called *Karina*. When the Colombian navy sunk the *Karina*, the M-19 had run out of resources.[51] Later in 1983 Bateman was killed in a plane crash in Panama which diminished the morale of the organization. This, in turn, provided an incentive to seek a political solution.

The M-19 signed a cease-fire agreement with the Colombian government in August 1984, which sparked a dialogue within the organization about how to transition into civilian life. Negotiations were hindered by the lack of any military presence of the M-19,[52] and it decided to establish a military training camp at Yarumales, a remote ridge in the Department of Cauca. In December 1984 the Colombian army attacked the training camp, but it was held off by the M-19 for twenty-two days. The M-19 leadership eventually decided to abandon this camp for an even smaller and more remote presence in Los Robles, two and a half miles away (and more than 1,300 feet higher in elevation). In response to the Yarumales attack, the top leadership was reorganized. At an M-19 conference in February 1985, Álvaro Fayad was promoted to the position of commander, and Carlos Pizarro (who had led the efforts to defend Yarumales) was unofficially second in command. The Central Committee was composed of Fayad, Pizarro, Iván Marino Ospina, Antonio Navarro Wolff, and Gustavo Arias. At this point the entire leadership of the M-19 was committed to negotiating a transition to civilian life.

Between February and June 1985 the Colombian army broke the agreed-upon cease-fire no less than three times, and the M-19 was able to hold it off militarily in every instance. But in May 1985 Navarro Wolff was injured, and the incentives (for the M-19) to unilaterally maintain the cease-fire had diminished. On June 20 the M-19 announced its return to

---

[51] De La Pedraja, *Wars of Latin America, 1948–1982.*
[52] The organization had very little to bargain with since it did not pose a credible military threat in this moment.

full military activity. It rearmed and engaged in several high-profile skirmishes in the summer and fall of 1985.[53]

On November 6, 1985, a contingent of at least thirty-five M-19 guerrillas took and occupied the Palace of Justice (the home of Colombia's Supreme Court) in Bogotá. By the morning of November 7, the building had been set ablaze, and virtually everyone still inside was dead, including twelve Supreme Court justices. This tragic event very much damaged the credibility of the M-19. And it would prove to be its last major military offensive. Nevertheless in recent years evidence has emerged to suggest that the Colombian army (with President Betancur's knowledge) took civilian hostages from the Palace of Justice on the first day of the siege and later tortured and murdered them. Moreover evidence indicates that the state forces knew in advance of the M-19's plans and allowed the siege to take place – that the situation was a "set up." In 2014 Retired General Jesús Armando Arias was convicted of ordering the forced disappearance of a judge, several court workers, and an M-19 guerrilla (Irma Franco Pineda) who had been seen leaving the building alive after the take-over.[54]

By July 1986 much of the top leadership of the M-19 had been killed (Ospina, Arias, and Fayad, as well as Andrés Almarales, Luís Otero, and Israel Santamaría). This left Carlos Pizarro and Antonio Navarro Wolff at the helm, and both were intellectual leaders who favored a political solution. Despite the fact that they continued military operations for two and a half more years, public enthusiasm for armed revolution and the military project of the M-19 had disappeared after the tragedy at the Palace of Justice.

In January 1988 the M-19 gathered all of its leadership and representatives from every political and military unit of the organization in a meeting that was called *Campo Reencuentro*,[55] where they agreed to suspend all military action. In October 1989 they voted almost unanimously to end the war, and in March 1990 almost 800 guerrillas handed over their weapons in a symbolic ceremony as they signed a formal peace accord with the government.[56]

---

[53] René de la Pedraja, *Wars of Latin America, 1982–2013* (Jefferson, NC: McFarland, 2013), 128–131.

[54] Woody, Christopher. "The Palace Siege: 30 Years since Rebel Fighters Launched a Devastating Attack on Colombia's Highest Court." *Business Insider*. Last modified November 7, 2015. www.businessinsider.com/colombia-palace-of-justice-siege-2015-11.

[55] Camp Reunion

[56] García Durán, Mauricio, Vera Grabe Lwewenherz, and Otty Patiño Hormaza. *M-19's Journey from Armed Struggle to Democratic Politics* (Berlin: Berghof Research Center for Constructive Conflict Management, 2008); De La Pedraja *Wars of Latin America, 1982–2013*, 135.

In April 1990 the leadership formed the Democratic Alliance (AD-M-19)[57] together with other progressive leaders as a new alternative political party. Soon after this, Pizarro (who was at the time running for president as the candidate of the AD) was assassinated, leaving only Antonio Navarro Wolff from the original leadership. Navarro Wolff ran for president in May and received more than 20 percent of the vote. In December the AD-M-19 elected nineteen deputies to the Constitutional Assembly. This represented the apex of the civilian party's influence. Because of the calculated repression as well as the pragmatic approach of Navarro Wolff, the party had all but disappeared by 1995.[58]

Mobilization Strategy during the First and Second Phases (1970–1996) – M-19

During its most active and successful years, the M-19 was a diverse and heterogeneous organization that had a diverse social and political platform that was informed by its youthful founders. The M-19 initially focused on its urban constituency because of its connections to ANAPO. Jaime Bateman's experience with the FARC and the Comuneros also influenced the platform and the mobilization strategy of the M-19 in its first decade of existence. Because of Bateman, land reform became an important rallying point for the M-19. There was a continual debate about the relative importance of building a broad-based (urban and rural) political base versus the importance of building up its military capacity for (rurally situated) combat with the Colombian army during this era. After the standoff at the Dominican Embassy in 1980, the M-19 moved its geographic focus to the poor and isolated Pacific coastal region of the country and mobilized campesinos in this area.

The ultimate goal of the M-19 throughout the 1980s was to negotiate a settlement with the government from a position of strength. As noted earlier, the M-19 established a broad-based political structure during the 1980s, which eventually resulted in its having a strong political-electoral presence in the early 1990s, including a larger presence than either

---

[57] *Alianza Democrática*
[58] Lawrence Boudon, "Colombia's M-19 Democratic Alliance: A Case Study in New-party Self-destruction." *Latin American Perspectives* 28 (2001): 73–92.

traditional political party in the Constituent Assembly that wrote the 1992 Colombian Constitution. At the height of its influence it represented a broad base of rural and urban interests across a broad range of popular social classes.

Ideology during the First Phase (1970–1982) – M-19

The M-19's political philosophy during the first phase was summarized in the formula "Democracy, Social Justice, and Anti-Imperialism," which proposed the construction of a revolutionary army – a "guerrilla of the masses" according to the expression used by its leader, Jaime Bateman Cayón at its 8th National Conference. It always represented a more moderate populist approach to armed revolution.

The general sociopolitical context in the country was complex in the late 1970s and early 1980s. Human rights violations committed during the presidency of Julio César Turbay Ayala (1978–1982) were well known by the international community. A Commission of Amnesty International visited the country in January 1980 and investigated reports of arbitrary arrests, torture, killings, and disappearances. The commission visited prisons, interviewed lawyers of political prisoners, families of detainees, and members of the armed forces and traveled to rural areas, and even met with the president. The government's response to the commission's report was to discredit the document, accusing it of trying to harm Colombia's international image. This deteriorating human rights situation impacted the evolving ideology of the M-19, which incorporated the more mainstream liberal ideology of the human rights regime, and thereby broadened its appeal among urban middle-class liberals and Leftists.[59] The M-19 was – for a time – the guerrilla group that most represented the ideals of a large and discontented sector of Colombian society.

Ideology during the Second Phase (1982–1996) – M-19

In 1984 a cease-fire and truce agreement was signed within the framework of Belisario Betancur's policy of peace. This signaled the willingness of the insurgent organizations to engage in dialogue.

---

[59] Because human rights are rooted in Western Enlightenment "liberal" ideology, the embracing of the language of human rights by armed revolutionary organizations often implied a softening of ideology.

The peace accord signed by the M-19 (and the EPL) and the national government in August 1984 represented a turning point with deep repercussions for the insurgent movement. Before the accord was signed, the M-19 had not limited its actions to the exercise of violence, but it had also undertaken the development of new practices of cultural promotion and political organization.

The presence of the M-19 in the peace process led to the creation of a group called *La Gaitana* Cultural Movement, which brought together people interested in promoting cultural activities in poor neighborhoods. Two militants, Lupe and Julian Serna, who were responsible for this collective project, represented the M-19. The group created the magazine *La Gaitana*, which published poems and literary writings of prominent local authors, and also the work of unknown writers who participated in writing workshops carried out in poor areas of the cities. The magazine also published pieces by Afranio Parra Guzmán, the national commander of the militia of the M-19, known for his passion for art and culture.[60]

The M-19 had broad public support because of its pluralistic and inclusive ideology. By the time it signed the peace accord, it was a broad-based movement stressing principles of social justice and liberal democracy. The middle classes, youths, and intellectuals sympathized with its struggles and operations, which explains why after its demobilization the M-19 received substantial electoral support, particularly in the election for representatives to the National Constituent Assembly in 1990. Consequently many of the causes the M-19 fought for were embodied in the Constitution of 1991. Unfortunately Carlos Pizarro, presidential candidate in the 1990 elections and leader of the movement, was assassinated in April 1990, thereby frustrating the hopes of broad sectors of the population.

THE TRANSITION OF THE ARMED STRUGGLE IN COLOMBIA

After negotiations with several armed movements were broken in 1985, the National Guerrilla Coordinating Body (CNG)[61] was created. It integrated the M-19, the Revolutionary Workers' Party (PRT), the Popular Liberation Army (EPL), the Quintin Lame Armed Movement, and the ELN. The FARC joined this group toward the end of 1987, which

---

[60] *La Gaitana*, Nos. 3–4, 1985, Hemeroteca Nacional.
[61] *Coordinadora Nacional Guerrillera*

led to the creation of the Simón Bolívar Coordinating Body (CGCS).[62] These alliances followed the example of other Latin American countries where armed movements were unified into a single front and under a Joint High Command (such as the URNG in Guatemala, the FMLN in El Salvador, and the FSLN in Nicaragua). The Simón Bolívar Guerrilla Coordinating Committee (CGSB) was formed in order to create a place for these revolutionary groups to coordinate their actions. The CGSB – for a time – represented the various constituent guerrilla organizations in their negotiations with the Colombian government. Little military-strategic coordination actually took place between the various guerrilla armies within the CGSB. By 1990, only the FARC, the ELN, and a dissident faction of the EPL still remained with the CGSB, as the other guerrilla organizations had demobilized by that point. And in 1991, the CGSB was completely disbanded. Nevertheless, the CGSB did effectively re-start the process of negotiating a political solution.

Colombian guerrilla groups also promoted larger legal political movements to get closer to social movements. The FARC created the UP; the ELN gave support to the movement *¡A Luchar!*[63]; and the M-19 eventually demobilized and formed a viable political party, the AD-M-19.

In general, it can be said that the armed revolutionary movements in Colombia led a guerrilla war of an ideological and political nature against the state, which took place in mostly rural areas. Its ultimate goal was the conquest of power for the people in order to build socialism. This was for a time the common objective for the FARC, ELN, and M-19. They followed different structural and ideological trajectories, and they recruited and were supported by different sectors of the population at different historical moments. Although they all aspired to become national movements, they all had a mostly regional character for the longer part of their histories. All of the armed movements of this era, like their Caribbean counterparts, were rife with internal divisions. They were all influenced by the polemical politics of the Cold War and drew on Marxist-Leninist doctrine at various stages. Nevertheless, at their roots, almost all of programs of the Colombian guerrillas can be classified as reformist. They all proposed changes in social relations without attempting to transform capitalism.[64]

According to Alejandro Reyes, the first strategic error of the Colombian state, which ended up enabling the emergence of the guerrillas

---

[62] *Coordinadora Guerrillera Simón Bolívar*   [63] To Struggle.
[64] Vargas, *Guerra o solución negociada*, 231.

in the 1960s, was "to use military repression to crush the peaceful demonstrations by campesino organizations, thus closing the reformist path."[65] Successive errors have been repeated by refusing to address the social problems that prompted and have kept alive the armed struggle in the country.

A notable study by historian Mauricio Archila states that in Colombia, between 1958 and 1990, 23.9 percent of social protests were motivated by issues related to the land, 16 percent to working conditions or lack of employment, 14 percent to violation of agreements or lack of sufficient regulating laws for social conflicts, 11 percent to poor provision of domestic public services, and 8 percent to the struggle for human rights.[66] The fracturing of the two-party system in Colombia[67] that coincided with the Cuban Revolution could have marked the rise of the popular movement and of a nonviolent political movement poised to implement significant social transformation (in a context of real democracy). But, unfortunately in response to this threat the ruling classes took actions to preserve the system that granted them privileges by taking advantage of their economic power and influence over the state.[68] Jaime Zuluaga has noted that despite the modernizing role of the National Front (1958–1974), which in practice seemed to last until the end of the 1980s, the Front "accentuated the gap between social and economic structures and political institutions, and strengthened and institutionalized the political tradition of exclusion. The exclusive nature of the two-party system agreement consolidated the elite interpretation of the opposition as subversive."[69]

Colombians have largely believed that because the country has not had military dictatorships (like many countries in the region), the political system is a "democracy." Despite the systematic use of violence by political

---

[65] Alejandro Reyes, *Guerreros y Campesinos. El despojo de la tierra en Colombia* (Bogotá: Friedrich Ebert Stiftung, Editorial Norma, 2008), 2.

[66] Mauricio Archila, *Idas y venidas, vueltas y revueltas. Protestas sociales en Colombia, 1958–1990* (Bogotá: CINEP, 2003), 234–235.

[67] The National Front was a power-sharing agreement between the Liberal and Conservative parties that was agreed to by the leadership of both parties. It was to last between 1958 and 1974. After 1974, the *de facto* agreement to include membership from the opposition party in the executive branch lasted until 1986.

[68] Camilo Posso, "Movimientos sociales y políticos en los años ochenta." *Revista Controversia* 141 (1987): 41.

[69] Jaime Zuluaga. "De guerrillas a movimientos políticos (análisis de la experiencia colombiana: el caso del M-19)," In *De las armas a la política*, compiled by Ricardo Peñaranda, and Javier Guerrero (Bogotá: IEPRI, 1999), 12.

and civil actors in Colombia, the legitimacy of elected presidential administrations has been respected, and transfers of executive power have been
handled peacefully through elections. During the twentieth century, there
was only one *coup d'état* (in 1953), partially approved by the political
elites.[70] However, rather than a real and substantive democracy, Colombia
has had what Guillermo O'Donnell called a "delegative democracy."[71]
The executive power overshadowed legislative power and was used to
justify harsh military responses, restricting individual rights, including the
right to strike, the right to freely mobilize, and the freedom of the press.[72]
Despite this, the myth of Colombian democracy has been deeply engrained
in the population, while the armed groups have become increasingly discredited by their affiliation with narco-trafficking and criminal networks.

The image of Colombia portrayed by the international media (particularly in the United States) is far removed from the country's reality.
Colombia's political reality is neither homogenous nor simultaneous
throughout the country. There have been regional and local areas that
have maintained highly democratic systems and culture, while there have
also been entire regions dominated by the right-wing paramilitary war-
lords and/or guerrillas.[73] This has created a political situation in which
most Colombians have had legitimate grievances that they have been
unable to articulate through democratic means, nor have they been able
to find recourse through armed struggle.

The armed struggle created a serious and devastating dilemma for
Colombians. Maintaining control over territory, justice, taxation, and
the official use of force is the purview of the state in any society, yet the
Colombian state has not successfully monopolized control over these
areas. According to Gonzalo Sánchez, a peculiarity of the Colombian
conflict (since the 1980s) is "the multiplicity of violence in terms of its
origins, objectives, geography, modus operandi and strategies." He adds,
"in the same scenario one can find organized crime, guerrilla warfare,
a dirty war and widespread violence."[74]

---

[70] Álvaro Tirado Mejía. "Rojas Pinilla: Del golpe de opinión al exilio." In *Nueva Historia de
Colombia*, ed. Alvaro Tirado Mejia (Bogotá: Editorial Planeta), 1989, 105–108.

[71] O'Donnell, Guillermo. "Delegative Democracy," *Journal of Democracy* 5:1 (January
1994): 55–69.

[72] Pedro Medellín. *El presidente sitiado. Ingobernabilidad y erosión de poder presidencial
en Colombia* (Bogotá: Editorial Planeta, 2006).

[73] Gustavo Duncan. *Los señores de la guerra* (Bogotá: Editorial Planeta, 2006), 36.

[74] Gonzalo Sánchez. "Guerra prolongada y negociaciones inciertas en Colombia."
In *Violencias y estrategias colectivas en la región andina*, ed. Gonzalo Sánchez and
Eric Lair (Bogotá: Editorial Norma, 2004), 22.

The end of the Cold War spelled the end of a particular paradigm and the international political and military support that had shaped and defined the armed revolutionary struggle in the Caribbean Basin. However, in the case of Colombia, armed groups found a way to survive, and the Colombian state was unwilling and unmotivated to negotiate a peace settlement until quite recently.[75] Thus over time, the war against drug trafficking in Colombia was conflated with the war against the armed insurgency. The alliance with illegal drug trafficking strengthened the remnants of the armed movements to the point that by the mid-1990s more than 40 percent of the revenues of the FARC came from the illegal drug business. Also, it is estimated that paramilitary groups that were fighting against the FARC received about 70 percent of their total income from narcotics trafficking. During these years, the state was unable to carry out its core functions. Because of this, there was an increase in both political and criminal violence – guerrillas, paramilitaries, drug traffickers, social cleansing groups, and common crime.[76] This made the goal of a negotiated peace ever more elusive over the course of the past three decades.

The infusion of drug trafficking into the civil-political conflict in Colombia turned it into what Jaime Zuluaga called "an ambiguous war." With the Colombian state, increasingly backed by the United States through Plan Colombia conflating the "war on drugs" (the state's attempt to tackle an entirely criminal enterprise) with the civil conflict, the political character of the guerrilla organizations began to be lost in the public understanding. This vision led to the criminalization of every adversary as a drug trafficker and a de-politicization of the conflict. Despite this public perception, both the FARC and the ELN are military organizations with political objectives; this has always left the door open for a political solution. Undermining this reality was both simplistic and self-defeating for the Colombian state. The FARC was marginalized and painted as a terrorist group funded by drug trafficking, and its real political platform – which has *always* been negotiable – was lost until quite recently.[77]

---

[75] Particularly under the administrations of Alvaro Uribe, who campaigned on and ruled with a "no negotiations" platform.

[76] Martha Cecilia García. "Luchas y movimientos cívicos en Colombia durante los años ochenta y los noventa. Transformaciones y permanencias." In *Movimientos sociales, Estado y democracia en Colombia*, ed. Mauricio Archila and Mauricio Pardo (Bogotá: Universidad Nacional de Colombia, Centro de Estudios Sociales, and Instituto Colombiano de Antropología e Historia, 2001), 99.

[77] Jaime Zuluaga. "Orígenes, naturaleza y dinámica del conflicto armado" In *Las otras caras del poder. Territorio, conflicto y gestión pública en municipios colombianos*, ed. Fabio Velásquez (Bogotá: Fundación Foro Nacional por Colombia, 2009), 50.

In the beginning, the Colombian conflict was an endogenous phenomenon – an internal war between Colombians. It evolved into a conflict that integrated the agendas of many multilateral interests. The conflict also resulted in a humanitarian crisis that has spilled over into neighboring countries. Between 1985 and 2002, more than 3 million people were uprooted from their homes, victims of the increasing violence.[78] Similarly the intensification of the conflict connected with major issues of the global agenda (drugs, human rights, migration, etc.) concerned every major global power.

PEACE PROCESS

In the late 1990s and during the government of conservative president Andrés Pastrana (1998–2002), a new process of political negotiations with the FARC was initiated. During these negotiations, the government allowed the FARC to control several municipalities in the southern part of the country. Unfortunately, the attempts at reconciliation were unsuccessful because the guerrillas used these clearance zones to strengthen their military capacity, and the popular political will began to turn against a negotiated solution. The guerrillas carried out multiple successful hits against the government by taking over towns and kidnapping members of the police and military, further eroding popular support for the negotiation process. The peace process was officially halted under the two-term administration of Álvaro Uribe (2002–2010). But when Uríbe's vice-president, Juan Manuel Santos, was elected to the presidency in 2010, he almost immediately began to lay the foundations for peace negotiations with the FARC by initiating secret and informal contacts. Formal negotiations began in November 2012 and were mediated by Norwegian and Cuban officials in Havana over the course of several years. The negotiations survived multiple setbacks, and a hard-fought reelection campaign in 2014 by Santos, which was considered by many as a referendum on the peace process. In August 2016 the two parties reached their final agreements, and the Colombian Congress ratified the accords in December 2016.[79]

---

[78] Marc Cherneck. *Acuerdo posible. Solución negociada al conflicto colombiano* (Bogotá: Ediciones Aurora, 2008).

[79] The original agreement called for a popular referendum in October 2016 to ratify the accords. The "No" campaign was spearheaded by Álvaro Uribe; after a well-funded and largely misleading campaign against the agreement, the referendum was not approved. The government and the FARC went back to the drawing board and modified the final agreement that was then ratified by Congress in December of the same year.

Finally, after fifty years of internal armed conflict, the FARC has laid down its weapons and this conflict is officially over. Although the ELN has not yet officially signed an agreement with the Colombian government, it appears as though this may be the opportunity for a lasting peace.

Suggested Reading

Archila, Mauricio. *Idas y venidas, vueltas y revueltas. Protestas sociales en Colombia, 1958–1990.* Bogotá: CINEP, 2003.

Arnson, Cynthia. *In the Wake of War: Democratization and Internal Armed Conflict in Latin America.* Stanford, CA: Stanford University Press, 2012.

Carrigan, Ana. *The Palace of Justice: A Colombian Tragedy.* New York: Four Walls, Eight Windows Press, 1993.

De La Pedraja, René. *Wars of Latin America, 1948–1982.* Jefferson, NC: McFarland, 2013.

De La Pedraja, René. *Wars of Latin America, 1982–2013.* Jefferson, NC: McFarland, 2013.

Grupo de Memoria Histórica. *Basta Ya! Colombia: Memorias de Guerra y Dignidad.* Bogotá: Imprenta Nacional, 2013.

Gustavo, Duncan. *Los señores de la guerra.* Bogotá: Editorial Planeta, 2006.

John Green, William. *Gaitanismo, Left Liberalism, and Popular Mobilization in Colombia.* Gainesville, FL: University Press of Florida, 2003.

Leech, Gary. *The FARC: The Longest Insurgency.* London: Zed Books, 2011.

Palacios, Marco. *Between Legitimacy and Violence: A History of Colombia, 1875–2002.* Durham, NC: Duke University Press, 2006.

Pecaut, Daniel. *Las FARC. ¿Una guerrilla sin fin o sin fines?* Bogotá: Editorial Norma, 2008.

Pizarro, Eduardo. *Una democracia asediada. Balance y perspectivas del conflicto armado en Colombia.* Bogotá: Grupo Editorial Norma, 2004.

Vargas, Alejo. *Guerra o solución negociada. ELN: origen, evolución y proceso de paz.* Bogotá: Intermedio Editores, 2006.

Villamizar, Dario. *Las guerrillas en Colombia: una historia desde los orígenes hasta los confines.* Bogotá: Editorial Debate. 2017.

Suggested Films

Colombia's Hidden Killers (2013)
50 Años en el Monte (1999)
El Baile Rojo (2003)
Falsos Positivos (2009)
Guerrilla Girl (2005)
Impunity (2014)

La Sierra (2004)
Los Guerrilleros Colombianos (2006)
No Hubo Tiempo para la Tristeza (2013)
Plan Colombia: Cashing-In on the Drug War Failure (2003)
Robatierras (2010)

6

Armed Organizations within the Puerto Rican Revolutionary Nationalist Movement

From the beginning of the twentieth century, Puerto Rico has been a dependency of the United States. This colonial situation has provoked dissent and opposition throughout the island's post-Spanish history. When the United States signed the Treaty of Paris with Spain in 1898, ending the Cuban war for independence (the Spanish-American war), Spain ceded all authority over Puerto Rico to the United States. US domination was reinforced in 1900 with the "Foraker law," which created a civilian government for Puerto Rico administered out of Washington, DC. In 1917 (in the wake of World War I), all Puerto Ricans were given US citizenship, and thus they could be drafted into military service. The net effect of these legal instruments was to establish Puerto Rico as a protectorate of the United States. Puerto Rico is a US territorial possession but does not form a part of the country. This second-class status continues to impact Puerto Rico's ability to engage in international trade. Because all ports of entry in Puerto Rico are technically US seaports, all trade to and from Puerto Rico is subject to the Jones Act of 1920. The Jones Act requires that all goods that are traded between US ports must be transported in US-made and US-owned vessels that are operated by a US-based merchant marine. This increases the costs for Puerto Rico to both import and export products to the United States. Additionally Puerto Rican men have been subject to selective service for more than 100 years, and they were drafted in large numbers in both World Wars and in the Vietnam War. In addition Puerto Rico has always been a popular vacation destination for US-based tourists, and so Puerto Rico has suffered from some of the same indignities that Cuba endured in the 1950s, as "America's playground."

There were three major phases of protest against the US presence on the island in the past century. The first stage occurred in the early twentieth century, but this resistance movement had no clear leadership or organization. Many Puerto Ricans viewed the US presence on the island as an illegitimate occupation, but their efforts at protest and resistance were mostly ineffectual and viewed as insignificant by US officials.[1] The second stage of anti-US opposition occurred between the 1930s and the 1950s. In this stage Pedro Albizu Campos and the Nationalist Party were the principal protagonists of the independence movement.[2] During those decades, in response to two prominent massacres (in Río Piedras in 1935 and in Ponce in 1937), a political movement and a publicity campaign were launched to denounce the US presence. This period included four important and distinct political acts of Puerto Rican nationalist protest: (1) the killing of the chief of police, Coronel Elisha Riggs, who was the official in charge of the slaughter at Río Piedras in 1935; (2) armed insurrections in October 1950 in Arecibo, Jayuya, Mayagüez, and Ponce; (3) the assault on Blair House, the provisional residence of the US president (Harry Truman) in 1954; and (4) the armed attack on the US Congress (also in 1954) by four young Puerto Rican separatists.[3]

From the 1950s until the middle of the 1980s, the third and most important phase of armed revolutionary protest occurred in Puerto Rico. This phase of armed opposition was referred to by the protagonists of the movement as the "*new* struggle for independence." During this stage the alliance between Puerto Rican Leftists and the revolutionary nationalist movement had a notable impact on the island and in the United States.

The aim of this chapter is to tell the story of the armed revolutionary movements in Puerto Rico during this latter period (the Cold War period). The four most important organizations during the period in question were the Pro-Independence Movement (MPI),[4] the Puerto Rican Socialist Party (PSP),[5] the Armed Commandos for Liberation (CAL),[6] and the

---

[1] Michael González Cruz, *Nacionalismo revolucionario puertorriqueño. La lucha armada, intelectuales y prisiones políticos y de guerra* (San Juan: Isla Negra Editores, 2006); José Paralitici, *La represión contra el independentismo puertorriqueño: 1960–2010* (San Juan: Publicaciones Gaviota, 2011).

[2] Albizu was also an important and aggressive labor leader and activist in Puerto Rico.

[3] For the last two events, the nationalists Andrés Figueroa Cordero, Irvin Flores Rodríguez, Lolita Lebrón, Rafael Cancel Miranda, and Oscar Collazo were imprisoned for several decades.

[4] *Movimiento Pro-Independencia*   [5] *Partido Socialista Puertorriqueño*
[6] *Comandos Armados de Liberación*

Revolutionary Workers Party-Puerto Rican Boricua Popular Army (PRTP-EPB).[7] Four other less significant organizations during this period will not be discussed here: the People's Armed Movement (MAP),[8] the Armed Forces of National Liberation (FALN),[9] the Armed Forces of Popular Resistance (FARP),[10] and the Volunteers' Organization for the Puerto Rican Revolution (OVRP).[11]

This third phase of armed resistance came to an end in part because of internal conflicts within the organizations. These organizations were also clearly impacted by the end of the Cold War and the collapse of socialism as a working revolutionary ideology. Unlike the other armed movements discussed in this book, the Puerto Rican armed movement was considered to be an essential part of the larger popular struggle to gain independence from the United States. Even though these guerrilla movements were unable to achieve independence, they did slowly give way to other non-violent forms of political and social participation that continue to advocate for autonomy from the United States.

NATIONAL AND INTERNATIONAL POLITICAL CONTEXT

The first point of analysis to consider with regard to the armed struggle in Puerto Rico is how external conditions (both regional and international) impacted the movement. The Cold War national liberation movements launched against the last vestiges of European colonialism throughout much of what was then called the "Third World," the Cuban Revolution, and the US intervention in Vietnam all formed a powerful set of circumstances that affected the birth and development of the guerrilla organizations in Puerto Rico. The influence of the global context was particularly important in shaping the methodology and the ideology used by Puerto Rican militants.

The US government met every political call for Puerto Rican independence with intense and violent repression. This repression was another factor that led to the choice of armed resistance by the militants. Throughout the entire course of its twentieth-century history, the struggle for emancipation was met with persecution; however, after the establishment of the Commonwealth of Puerto Rico (*Estado Libre y Asociado*) in 1952, violent repression of any and all efforts to assert independence

---

[7] *Partido Revolucionario de los Trabajadores Puertorriqueños-Ejército Popular Boricua*
[8] *Movimiento Armado del Pueblo*   [9] *Fuerzas Armadas de Liberación Nacional*
[10] *Fuerzas Armadas de Resistencia Popular*
[11] *Organización de Voluntarios Por la Revolución Puertorriqueña*

increased dramatically. During these decades, especially in the 1970s, persecution (arrests and killings) of supporters of independence became increasingly common. Starting in the 1960s the FBI initiated a program to infiltrate political, trade union, and student organizations. This counter-intelligence program also involved wire-tapping phone calls and inter-cepting mail communications, massive public disinformation campaigns, and even targeted bombings on the island. In its efforts to crush groups that called for independence, the FBI collaborated with Puerto Rican police forces, the US Coast Guard, the CIA, the US army and extremist right-wing groups that included Cuban exile groups.[12] The armed response by Puerto Rican militants was a direct response to the violence that emanated from the dominant powers in authority.

Also, during the Vietnam conflict, there was vocal and public resistance to compulsory military service (the draft) in Puerto Rico, as there was on the mainland. The insertion of an ROTC program at the University of Puerto Rico also provoked radical opposition. The larger protest move-ment surrounding the Vietnam War had a radicalizing impact on the movement for independence. The issues of independence, the Vietnam War, opposition to mining on the island, protests against the presence of US military bases and demands for the release of political prisoners were conflated during this period.

In contrast to many of the other armed movements in the Caribbean Basin, armed struggle in Puerto Rico did not involve distinct phases. Because the question of independence was a long-standing issue in Puerto Rico, and because the urban character of the movement never really changed, the armed struggle in Puerto Rico evolved in the same way throughout the entire Cold War period. This distinguishes this movement from its counterparts in Central America and Colombia, where the structures, tactics, and ideologies evolved in distinct phases. Nevertheless it is possible to discuss the same variables within these organizations that we outlined previously.

INTERNAL STRUCTURE OF THE GROUPS

With the notable exception of the People's Armed Movement (MAP), a rural militia that emerged in the mountainous northwest of the island, the

---

[12] Ramón Bosque Pérez, and José Colón Morera, *Las Carpetas. Persecución política y derechos civiles en Puerto Rico* (Río Piedras: Centro para la Investigación y Promoción de los Derechos Civiles, 1997); José Paralitici, *La represión contra el independentismo puertorriqueño: 1960–2010* (San Juan: Publicaciones Gaviota, 2011).

guerrilla groups in Puerto Rico were all distinctly urban. Although they initially tried to create a rural vanguard *foco* (similar that in Cuba), this strategy quickly ended in failure. The commitment to armed struggle, however, did not so easily disappear.

Internal Structure of the MPI-PSP

One of the first groups to take up arms was the Pro-Independence Movement (MPI).[13] Though it did not initially organize as a guerrilla army, the founders and leaders of this organization recognized that violence would likely be inevitable in the struggle for the emancipation. This organization was founded in 1959 by a group of dissidents from the Puerto Rican Independence Party (PIP),[14] former militants of the Communist Party of Puerto Rico, and other nationalist groups. In its beginning, the group adopted a "nonpartisan position" agreement with two established political groups – the League of Patriots of Eugenio Hostos and the Pro Independence Congress.

The goal of the organization's leadership was to spearhead a multi-class coalition composed of every group that favored independence. However, there were divisions within the MPI that became evident soon after its inception. One of the principal leaders of the MPI, Juan Mari Brás, advocated that the MPI should endorse the candidate promulgated by the PIP. He justified this position as a mere "tactical question," which would not have long-term implications for the movement. The other important leader of the MPI, John A. Corretjer, called for abstention from the election as a matter of principle. This had been the position of the older Nationalist Party. This issue, together with public differences about the significance of the Cuban Revolution, prompted Corretjer and his group to withdraw from the MPI during its Second National Assembly in 1960.[15]

In those years the movement was organized into various functional "missions" or branches. The leadership was formed by a General Assembly (*Secretariado General*) composed of ninety elected representatives who in turn elected a directorate (la *Misión Nacional*), composed of

---

[13] This book considers the MPI-PSP as part of a single historical current.

[14] *Partido Independentista Puertorriqueño*

[15] Juan Mari Bras, *El independentismo en Puerto Rico. Su pasado, su presente y su porvenir* (Santo Domingo: Editorial Cepa, 1984), 132.

seventeen leaders. Juan Mari Brás was elected as the secretary general of the organization from the outset, and he remained in that position for several years. In addition to publishing a newspaper, *Claridad*, the group had a weekly bulletin that reported on the internal affairs of the movement. In 1962 in Mari Brás's first political manifesto titled *The Hour of the Independence*, the MPI was defined as "a patriotic vanguard" whose aim was to emancipate the nation through multiple fronts, including armed force.

Mari Brás's public statement of his willingness to used armed struggle provoked enormous debate within the base of the MPI, as well as in other political movements on the island. This debate often turned on the question of the viability and/or necessity of defending the Cuban Revolution, together with a polarizing discussion of the use of guerrilla warfare. In the context of this debate, the level and intensity of youth protests against the Vietnam War and the draft were increasing. This had the effect of radicalizing both the tactics and the rhetoric of the movement. At the Seventh National Assembly of the MPI in 1968 it was stated: "armed struggle is one means for the Puerto Rican people to confront the Yankee empire in order to achieve independence and national liberation."[16]

A year later (in 1970) these ideas were promulgated in a new political manifesto: *Present and Future of Puerto Rico: The Doctrine of the New Struggle for Independence*. Here MPI outlined the need to "use Marxism-Leninism as a guide to action" and the right to "resort to armed struggle" to achieve independence from the United States. At the same time the document proposed five organizing principles that should govern the MPI: "democratic centralism, collective action, organizational discipline, reviews of agreements and critique and self-criticism."[17]

These changes also affected the relationship between the labor movement and the struggle for independence. In 1969–1970, a difficult and prolonged strike by workers at General Electric in Palmer (Río Grande) involved the aggressive participation of the MPI. After this incident the MPI began systematic trade-union work. During the 1971 May Day labor celebration, Mari Brás announced in *Claridad* MPI's decision to become the party that the Puerto Rican working class would use to take power.[18] A few months later in November, at the Eighth National Assembly of the MPI, it founded the Puerto Rican Socialist Party (PSP). Several factors

---

[16] *Claridad*, May 5, 1968.
[17] Wilfredo Mattos Cintrón, *Puerta sin casa: Crisis del PSP y encrucijada de la izquierda* (San Juan: La Sierra Editores, 1984), 18–19.
[18] Ibid., 25.

explain the transformation of the organization from a multi-class broad-front coalition supporting independence to a socialist revolutionary organization. These factors include the rise of campus protests, increased demands of the trade unions, the divisions within the PIP that emerged when it confronted more radical elements, and the growing sympathy within the movement for Cuba-inspired revolutionary socialism in the region.

At the time that it was formed, the General Declaration of the PSP enumerated four basic rights that defined its struggle: (1) independence and sovereignty, (2) the need to recover the Puerto Rican heritage that had been yielded to "foreign persons, corporations, governments or forces," (3) the right to "the progressive socialization of all the means of production" and to the construction "of a socialist society," and (4) the right to use "all forms of struggle" including "revolutionary violence against repressive violence."[19]

Based on these principles, the PSP wrote the following in the preamble to its constitution:

To be the revolutionary vanguard of the people of Puerto Rico and to bring together the most conscious members of the working class with other segments of society who can adopt a proletarian ideology in concert with the principles of Marxism-Leninism in order to lead the nation in its struggle for independence and towards the establishment of a Democratic Republic of the Workers ... these are the first steps towards the construction of socialism.[20]

The PSP instituted as symbols a red flag in a rectangular shape with a white five-pointed star in the upper left-hand corner and a shield with a black circle in the shape of a gear with a black fist in the bottom, along with the name of the organization. The "International" (the anthem of the Communist International or Comintern) was often sung in its mass meetings along with the Puerto Rican national anthem, *La Borinqueña*. *Claridad* was named the "journalistic organ" of the PSP and the Central Committee of the PSP was charged with appointing the editorial control of the magazine.[21]

The members of the PSP were distinguished as either *militantes* or *afiliados*. The "militants" were required to ascribe to all party documents

[19] Partido Socialista Puertorriqueño, *Declaración General del PSP* (Rio Piedras: Ediciones Puerto Rico, 1972), 55–56.
[20] Partido Socialista Puertorriqueño, *Reglamento* (Rio Piedras: Ediciones Puerto Rico, 1974 [b]).
[21] Ibid.

and to (1) engage in "activities that furthered the struggle for independence and also socialism"; (2) subordinate themselves "to the discipline of the party and to the interests of the working class, and its affiliates, including union organizing, student politics, or cultural manifestations; ... and (3) be over the age of 16 and to have been an active member for at least six months." Militants were asked to attend all Party meetings. They were eligible to elect and/or to be elected as leaders in any level of the organization. They were allowed to take part in discussions and the formulation of the political platform of the party. "Affiliate" members were not required to adopt the same level of discipline and commitment as militants. Nevertheless affiliates were also required to act in the interests of the party to the best of their abilities. Affiliates were allowed the right to attend and participate in party activities but only in an *ex officio* capacity.[22]

The structure of the PSP was based on the Leninist principles of "democratic centralism." The vertical structure of the PSP was organized around subgroups: the local cells (*nucleos*), the Assembly of Cells, the local Committees, the Assembly of Committees, the "Zone" Committees, the Assembly of Zone Committees, the Central Committee, and the National Congress. The cell was the heart of party membership, and cells were established in places of work, in schools and universities, and in neighborhoods and communities. Members in the cells were to meet at least once a week and to carry out planned activities and collect the contributions of the members. The Central Committee was the most important authoritative body during the intervals between congressional assemblies. The Central Committee was tasked with the dissemination of the party platform, strengthening and enforcing ideological unity, and exercising any required disciplinary actions. They were also responsible for forging alliances with other parties and for appointing the members of the "Political Commission." The Political Commission always included the Secretary General (who was the acting spokesperson), the President (the official representative of the party), and the Secretary of Organization (who was the head of the organizational tasks or the horizontal organization of the party). In practice the Political Commission functioned as the ruling body for the day-to-day operations of the party.[23]

Toward the end of 1975, the organization had 2,635 affiliate members, at least 14,300 sympathizers, and 1,056 militants. It had an organized presence in sixty municipalities and 238 political organizations.[24] A few

---

[22] Ibid.   [23] Ibid.

[24] Ángel Agosto, *Lustro de gloria* (San Juan: La Casa Editora de Puerto Rico, 2009), 180.

years later, as a result of its internal crises, these numbers were significantly diminished. The most significant issue was a fundamental disagreement about the political strategy of the party. On the one hand the PSP was clandestinely preparing for armed struggle; at the same time the organization was focusing attention and the bulk of its resources on electoral activism. Hector Meléndez, one of the main leaders of the party, reflected that throughout its short history the PSP had to manage two conflicting tendencies. It saw itself as a revolutionary body, disposed to an armed insurrection of the working class, and also in "legalistic" terms, which is to say that it actively sought engagement with the official sphere.[25] The underlying tension between these two identities created a series of crises and ruptures between 1976 and 1982. At the end of the 1980s the organization fell apart and with it the vision of a revolutionary workers party engaged in armed struggle.

Internal Structure of the CAL

The Armed Commandos for Liberation (CAL) surfaced in 1968 as a result of a series of articles published in *Claridad*. Although it had begun to carry out activities in the previous year, it decided to announce its formation publicly on the occasion of the anniversary of the "Cry of Lares."[26] In its first communiqué it announced that its mission was exclusively directed at the "imperialist enemy" that had "infiltrated all aspects of Puerto Rican national life." Its stated goal then was independence through the expulsion of the "yankee invader and its capitalist imperialist allies."[27]

The CAL was organized into a tightly disciplined clandestine and military organization from the beginning to avoid being attacked by local police and security forces or the US military. Its internal structure was also determined on the basis of the Leninist principle of democratic centralism. As such, it too had a General Assembly, a National Directorate, and a Central Command unit. The General Assembly was the ultimate authority within the CAL, tasked with all political decisions. During the interim between Assembly gatherings, the National Directorate conducted all of the business of the organization. The

---

[25] Héctor Meléndez, *El fracaso del proyecto PSP de la pequeña burguesía* (Río Piedras: Editorial Edil, 1984), 11.

[26] The *Grito de Lares* (or the Lares Uprising) is the name given to the revolutionary movement that Puerto Ricans launched against Spain. The uprising took place in the town of Lares on September 23, 1868.

[27] *Claridad*, February 25, 1968.

Central Command unit was in charge of the overall management of the organization.[28]

In a document published in *Claridad* the organization explained that it was organized according to a "Command Structure" (*Comandancia*) whereby all political-military objectives and actions were discussed and then carried out. It also indicated that it was organized into three "sections": (1) intelligence, (2) supplies and technical issues, and (3) actions. The first section was tasked with gathering intelligence on the official security measures adopted by the "repressive apparatus." It was also responsible for analyzing the risks of its own actions to the civilian population. The second section was responsible for learning to make and use explosive devices. And the third detachment was composed of armed combatants who were tasked with physically carrying out the military operations of the organization.[29] By 1974 the CAL decided to dissolve the organization. This did not, however, lead to the end of organized armed resistance on the island, as other groups continued with the struggle.

Internal Structure of the PRTB-EPB – Macheteros

The Puerto Rican Revolutionary Workers Party- Boricua Popular Army (PRTP-EPB), popularly known as the *Macheteros*, can best be understood through its intimate connection with the life of its founder and commander Filiberto Ojeda Ríos.[30] Ojeda began his political career within the Carlos Pelegrín García Liberation Movement[31] in New York. This organization was created to defend the rights of Puerto Ricans in the United States and to struggle against racial discrimination. By the end of the 1950s it had allied with Fidel Castro's 26th of July Movement and its allied organization in New York.[32]

By the middle of the 1960s, inspired by the successful Cuban Revolution, Ojeda moved his base of operations to Cuba. It was there that he joined the Cuban section of the MPI. In 1968 he represented the MPI at the first Transcontinental Conference (OSPAAAL) in

---

[28] Lucila Irizarry Cruz, *CAL: una historia clandestina* (San Juan: Isla Negra Editores, 2010), 81–83.

[29] *Claridad*, June 4, 1972.

[30] At least this is so, until his murder by the FBI on September 23, 2005.

[31] *Movimiento Libertador de Carlos Pelegrín García*

[32] Luis Nieves Falcón, *Conversaciones con Filiberto Ojeda Ríos: La Luz de la Ventana* (San Juan: Ediciones Puerto, 2002).

Havana.[33] During this period Ojeda developed a strong relationship with many important Latin American revolutionary leaders and thinkers, including Fidel Castro, Che Guevara, Amilcar Cabral, and Salvador Allende.

At the end of the 1960s he formed the Revolutionary Independence Movement in Arms (MIRA).[34] The purpose of this organization was to set up a base of operations, both on the island and in the continental United States to demonstrate against the colonial situation of Puerto Rico. After a series of arrests, including that of Ojeda himself, the group disbanded. Ojeda, however, continued to promote his revolutionary cause through other channels.

Ojeda decided to establish closer ties with working class organizations and with poor communities. He hoped to both support their struggles while expanding his own base of support. Ojeda's organization edited the newspaper *El Martillo* ("The Hammer"), which provided an important political platform for the movement. At the same time it began to form alliances and to act in concert with other armed groups in Puerto Rico (i.e., CAL, the FARP, and the OVRP). As a product of this experience, in July 1976 the Macheteros were born. The EPB (the Borriqua Popular Army) was the wing of the organization responsible for armed operations, and the PRTP (Puerto Rican Revolutionary Workers Party) was the political wing. Among its first militant members were former members of CAL, the PSP, and the MIRA.

There is very little reliable information about the internal organization of the Macheteros. And despite their official organizational structure, the Macheteros were tightly controlled and directed by a Directorate Committee, which was in turn controlled by Ojeda.

The actions of the Macheteros were nurtured by the experiences of other urban guerrilla movements such as the Tupamaros of Uruguay. Like the other urban guerrilla organizations in Puerto Rico and in Latin America, the clandestine structure of the organization was modeled on the principle of democratic socialism. The PRTP-EPB engaged in a broad range of both paramilitary and legal political activity. The militants of the organization came from diverse backgrounds and as such they ascribed to diverse ideological principles. It is worth mentioning that women militants took many leading roles within the organization, and they were

---

[33] First Tricontinental Conference of the *Organización de Solidaridad con Asia, África y América Latina.*

[34] *Movimiento Independentista Revolucionario en Armas*

actively involved in both the political and military actions of the Macheteros.

It is also important to note that the Macheteros did not limit their activities to armed struggle. They sought to create a workers' party that emanated from the labor movement. Because of their clandestine nature, we know little about this political activity, but we do know (from their communiqués and public statements) that they were deeply involved in this type of political work and labor organizing.

The PRTP-EPB did act in coordination with other clandestine groups. In one instance it carried out an armed assault in Sabana Seca, together with the FARP and the OVRP. Also, on July 25, 1979, in commemoration of the anniversary of the North American invasion of the island, the FALN in Chicago publicly declared its political alliance with the FARP, the OVRP, and the Macheteros.

Despite the efforts to coordinate a unified alliance between the clandestine groups, the organization split into two factions in 1984. Jorge Farinacci led the PRT-Macheteros and Ojeda took the leadership of the EPB-Macheteros. According to several protagonists of the movement, the reasons for the split were complicated and included "distinct visions of the struggle" as well as personality differences.

In August 1985, after a series of betrayals and infiltrations of the group, several militants were arrested, including Ojeda. These arrests effectively ended all activity of the organization.

MOBILIZATION STRATEGIES OF THE ORGANIZATIONS

Mobilization strategies in the Puerto Rican case differed from the other cases because of the primarily urban nature of the movement. The literal quest for liberation (independence from the United States) also impacted the development and evolution of the mobilization strategies in all of the organizations being analyzed here.

Mobilization Strategy of the MPI

The MPI from its beginnings was conceived as a national liberation movement, and it was deeply inspired by the ideas of the Puerto Rican nationalist Pedro Albizu Campos, as well as the twentieth-century anti-colonial leaders of Asia and Africa. Its base was mobilized by appealing to nationalist and anti-colonialist sentiments that were prevalent within Puerto Rican society. The organization developed its mobilization strategy in several ways. It built a substantial membership base by organizing massive protest campaigns against the Vietnam War and Selective Service (the draft) in Puerto Rico. It generally opposed involvement in the electoral process but did use extensive internal and international channels (including legal official channels) to continually denounce the colonial status of Puerto Rico. And it was not uncommon for the MPI to carry out this political work in concert with other political parties and groups, including the PIP.

The demand for Puerto Rican emancipation was intimately connected to support for the Cuban Revolution. After some internal debate the MPI officially adopted a pro-Cuba (anti-US) position. In the middle of the 1960s the MPI established a permanent presence (mission) in Cuba. Some of its militants took political courses and received military training in Cuba as well. The relationship between the MPI and the Cuban Revolution had an impact on whom they recruited and how they were recruited as well.

Mobilization Strategy of the PSP

From the outset, the PSP was formed to advance the struggle of the Puerto Rican working class. It participated in labor and trade union protests; and on some occasions it provided armed support to workers during violent labor conflicts.[35]

As a consequence of the radicalization of the working class and the student movement, in 1971 the General Declaration of the party established the following:

It is now necessary for all of the combatants in the struggle for independence and socialism to be prepared to move rapidly and effectively from an open struggle to a clandestine one, and from a legal plane to illegality; and that they all be prepared to respond to the repressive violence of the regime with revolutionary violence should the circumstances call for it.[36]

Furthermore, during the First Extraordinary Congress of 1974 the need to use "armed force to the defeat the enemy" was reiterated.[37] Similarly, an ex-militant of the PSP claimed that in 1975 the party created an "armed unit" with 247 members organized in six columns distributed across the

---

[35] Agosto, Lustro de gloria, 22.
[36] Partido Socialista Puertorriqueño, *Declaración General del PSP* (Rio Piedras: Ediciones Puerto Rico, 1972), 91.
[37] Partido Socialista Puertorriqueño, *La Alternativa Socialista. Tesis política* (Carolina: Impresora nacional, 1974[a]), 174.

island. He also described how this military "infrastructure" assisted the striking workers of the newspaper *El Mundo* by delivering explosives that were used to destroy the helicopters that the company was using to intimidate the picketers and to transport strike breakers.[38]

The organization also continued the tradition established by the Nationalist Party and the MPI of mobilizing and organizing Puerto Rican militants within the continental United States. In an official document of the North American organization of the PSP (*Desde las Entrañas*), the PSP also restated the need for armed struggle.[39]

During the Second Socialist Congress in 1975, the PSP made a tactical decision to participate in the 1976 general elections.[40] Though this resolution was respected, it generated substantial controversy. The organization's focus on an electoral strategy came at the expense of its other activist fronts and its commitment to armed struggle.

The controversy and conflict within the PSP was aggravated by the resounding electoral defeat. Internal divisions and difficulties were accelerated, creating a genuine crisis within the organization. Despite this the PSP decided to participate in the 1980 election as well. Although its candidate did better in these elections, the discord surrounding the electoral strategy continued.

At the Third Congress of 1982, the leadership of the party concluded that its priority was no longer the formation of a revolutionary workers' party, but rather a "multiclass patriotic movement for national salvation."[41] This decision was polarizing, and after this the PSP lost membership and influence until it eventually folded in 1992.

Mobilization Strategy of the CAL

The leadership of the CAL focused its military activities on the American presence on the island, especially military bases and US corporations. It

---

[38] Agosto, Lustro de gloria, 156–157; see also *Claridad*, February 10, 1972. "Infrastructure" is a term that was used in the epoch to refer to the armed apparatus of the organization.

[39] *Claridad* was published and distributed in a bilingual weekly edition in the United States from its beginnings in 1972. Its autonomy and editorial freedom were always recognized by the Central Committee. See Partido Socialista Puertorriqueño, "Desde las Entrañas," *Revista Nueva Lucha,* January–February, 1974(c).

[40] These were elections for both the Governor of Puerto Rico, as well as for senators and congressional representatives.

[41] Héctor Meléndez, *El fracaso del proyecto PSP de la pequeña burguesía* (Río Piedras: Editorial Edil, 1984), 37.

denounced the economic, political, and military monopolies of the United States and opposed the economic forces that pressured Puerto Ricans to emigrate. Alfonso Beal, the public spokesperson for the CAL, said the following in a report published in the *Bulletin Tri-continental*:

Our actions are aimed at undermining the colonial stability and the peace of our imperialist invaders; we are only in the first stage of operations, and in this phase we intend to cause $100 million worth of damage to US concerns ...

We begin our struggle by linking our actions to the problems of the working class and the people in general who are affected by the imperialist presence here ... when the telephone workers' strike broke out last April we were mobilized in solidarity with the striking workers to sabotage the company – a subsidiary of the ITT monopoly.[42]

Following this same pattern CAL carried out attacks on North American companies such as Franklins, Bakers, Sears, and K-Mart. As a part of this strategy, the group declared the tourist area of Condado as a "war zone," warning Puerto Ricans to stay away from this "center of vice and corruption."[43] It claimed that the area had become a "refuge for gangsters and the American mafia as well as Cuban *gusanos* [worms]."[44]

In another instance, it attacked the Cataño pipelines that transported oil to the US Air Force Base in Ramey (Aguadilla). It also sabotaged the communication centers of the Roosevelt Roads Naval Station in Ceiba and the Army Officers' Club in San Juan. The CAL also raided several mining quarries to steal explosive materials.

Finally, the organization actively participated in several prominent labor conflicts with the workers of the *Hipódromo El Comandante* (the race track), the Puerto Rico Telephone Company, General Electric, the New York Department Store, and the newspaper *El Mundo*. Its political posture was neatly summarized in the following communiqué:

Our armed forces have a fundamental duty to stand in active solidarity with our exploited working class. The *Boricua* worker – creator of the wealth that the foreigners usurp from us – must be respected; the struggles for vindication carried out by our proletariat provide encouragement to all of the commandos. Many of us are members of the working class – and we reaffirm our commitment to assist the workers' struggles in every way that we can.[45]

The CAL never attacked the local civilian population; on the contrary, its strategy of urban guerrilla warfare created solidarity – tacit

---

[42] Interview with Alfonso Beal. See Gaspar Cúneo Elizondo, "No somos el brazo armado de una organización determinada." *Boletín Tricontinental*, 1968.
[43] *Claridad*, January 24, 1971.   [44] Ibid.   [45] *Claridad*, September 20, 1970.

and explicit – from diverse sectors of Puerto Rican society. The pro-nationalist message garnered the support of small businesspeople, shopkeepers, and ordinary citizens who provided information about the intelligence gathering being carried out by the police and the FBI. Residents from smaller towns outside of San Juan as well as various workers' organizations were publicly grateful to the CAL for its actions. The only action by CAL that cost lives involved two US Navy men in San Juan. This was taken in reprisal for the police murder of a student, Antonia Martínez Lagares.[46] This is how CAL defended this incident:

We will defend any and all groups and independence leaders when the circumstances require our intervention. For example, when the police killed the student Antonia Martínez, we took reprisal, liquidating two members of the Yankee Navy (though the press only reported one). In the same way we will do this every time there is a threat, an injury or an assassination of a Puerto Rican patriot. We will always respond quickly, and it will always be a *yanqui* or *pitiyanqui*[47] who pays the price for every act of aggression against our independence fighters.[48]

Even though the CAL publicly claimed that it was *not* the armed wing of any other political group, on several occasions articles published in *Claridad* indicated that CAL and the MPI-PSP had a close organizational relationship. Testimonies of former militants as well as other witnesses corroborate this. It was well known that the name of CAL's public spokesperson ("Beal") was fictitious, and that it was drawn from the first syllables of the surnames of two historically important leaders of the Puerto Rican independence movement – Ramon *Be*tances and Pedro *Al*bizu. "Beal" was a personage who embodied the collective identity of the National Direction of the armed group. Nevertheless the pseudonym was real enough for student protesters in the 1960s and 1970s who were known to chant *Alfonso Beal! Puerto Rico quiere CAL!* (Alfonso Beal! Puerto Rico wants CAL!).[49]

---

[46] The young woman was murdered by the police during student protests against the presence of a North American ROTC program on the Río Piedras campus of the University of Puerto Rico in March 1970.

[47] "Pitiyanqui" is a derogatory term given to a Puerto Rican who acted servile or deferent to non-Hispanic North Americans. A "pityanqui" is ashamed of his Puerto Rican heritage. The term has its origins in Puerto Rico of the 1940s and 1950s.

[48] *Claridad*, November 22, 1970.

[49] Denis Manuel Maldonado, *Hacia una interpretación marxista de la historia de Puerto Rico y otros ensayos* (Río Piedras: Editorial Antillana, 1977), 289.

Mobilization Strategy of the PRTB-EPB – Macheteros

The Macheteros delineated three distinct types of operations that they engaged in during these years. First they were committed to responding to state-sponsored violence when it was directed toward members of the broader movement for independence. Second they performed symbolic acts to denounce the colonial regime. And finally they expropriated property that could be used in the struggle. Their commitment to this operational strategy largely determined who would be mobilized into the organization. Although this categorization generally describes the actions taken by the group, the actions themselves often served a diverse range of purposes. For example, after the murders of two young members of the independence movement in Cerro Maravilla, the Macheteros ambushed a police patrol. This act allowed them to take the police weapons while taking revenge for the crime committed by the security forces.[50] Similarly, in December 1979, the Macheteros attacked a US navy vehicle in Sabana Seca, killing two marines and injuring nearly a dozen more; this was done in response to the murder of an activist who had been imprisoned for defending Vieques.[51] They explained the motive for the attack in a communiqué:

The imperialistic aggressions against our people have been a constant, and in recent years they have culminated in the massacre of two young patriots in the Cerro Maravilla. And more recently a young farmworker and patriot, Ángel Rodríguez Christopher, was assassinated in Tallahassee's federal dungeons ... [They warn then that] the blood of the *Boricua* martyrs and patriots will be paid for with the blood of the imperialists.[52]

The Macheteros staged important symbolic actions during these years to advance the goal of emancipation and to demonstrate their opposition to the use of Puerto Rican territory as a US military base of operations in the Caribbean. The group fired an M-72 rocket at the offices of the FBI in Hato Rey in October 1983 (during the US invasion of Granada) in an action of "fraternal solidarity with the brotherly people of Granada."[53] In January 1985 they launched a missile at the US Federal Court House in old San Juan.

One of the most significant actions (called "Pitirre II") taken by the Macheteros was the attack against the Muñiz Air National Guard Base in

---

[50] In July 1978 the FBI and police executed two young Puerto Rican separatists after laying a trap. This caused a massive outcry by the local population.

[51] Angel Rodríguez Cristobal was the militant member of the Puerto Rican Socialist League who was murdered in prison.

[52] *Claridad*, December 7, 1979.   [53] *Claridad*, November 4, 1983.

Isla Verde on January 11, 1981. They destroyed eight Corsair A7D combat jets and were able to deactivate an F104, with no victims. The organization justified this highly symbolic operation by arguing that this air base was where US fighter planes took off to invade Granada.[54] It also speculated that the base would be used to launch an attack on the FMLN in El Salvador.[55]

Finally, the Macheteros launched one their boldest and most consequential actions when they robbed more than $7 million from a Wells Fargo facility in Hartford, Connecticut, in 1983. Two years later the FBI made numerous arrests in different cities in Puerto Rico, the United States, and Mexico in connection with that armed robbery. Fourteen Machetero militants were arrested, including several important leaders.[56]

The Macheteros also used a tactic known as "armed propaganda." On January 6, 1985 as part of the festivities surrounding "Three Kings Day" (the Epiphany),[57] the Macheteros distributed gifts to hundreds of Puerto Rican children in Hartford, as well as in Puerto Rico, using part of the money they obtained in the Wells Fargo robbery.[58]

Like the other armed groups in Puerto Rico, the Macheteros accompanied workers during the telephone workers' strikes and in other community-based protests. They were especially involved in the efforts of the Vieques community to push out the US.[59] The communities in Vieques strongly identified with the Macheteros who stood in solidarity with them. The Macheteros often protected the citizens of Vieques from the police. The Macheteros also had support within the judiciary and the Puerto Rican police forces. In fact, when the FBI launched high profile investigations of the Macheteros (i.e., Ojeda's murder in 2005) they intentionally excluded native Puerto Rican agents.

The Puerto Rican community in the United States also offered solidarity in several different forms to the Macheteros. They provided housing and employment, and offered assistance for the legal defense of militants who were arrested. After the arrests and imprisonments of 1985, several solidarity groups were formed both in Puerto Rico and in the mainland

---

[54] See *La Voz Obrera*, September 1998.

[55] Communiqué of Boricua Popular Army – Macheteros, see *Claridad*, January 16, 1981.

[56] Ronald Fernández, *Los Macheteros: El robo a la Wells Fargo y la Lucha Armada por la Independencia de Puerto Rico* (Río Piedras: Editorial Edil, 1993).

[57] It is customary for Puerto Ricans to celebrate the Epiphany with parades, festivals, and family gatherings. Traditionally children received presents on January 6 rather than on Christmas day.

[58] *Claridad*, January 11, 1985.   [59] *Claridad*, February 13, 1981.

US. They eventually came together to form the Committee against Repression Unit (CUCRE) and the National Committee for Freedom of Political Prisoners and War (CNPLPPG).

IDEOLOGIES OF THE ORGANIZATIONS

As was the case with all of the revolutionary movements in the Caribbean Basin, ideology was in some measure determined by the structures and tactics of the organizations. In particular, both the struggle for independence from the United States and the urban character of the movement significantly influenced the ideological trajectory. The Puerto Rican movements were also influenced by classic Leninist ideology and their alliances with urban workers and trade unions. Nevertheless, there was always significant ideological diversity within the movement, and this did cause division and conflict in some instances.

Ideology of the MPI-PSP

The ideology of the MPI-PSP evolved and adapted during the turbulent years of its existence. It was also true that at any given time the militants of the MPI-PSP ascribed to a diverse range of philosophies and ideologies.

From its beginning, the central objective for the MPI-PSP was independence. In some sense the organization was born as an alliance of all the different ideological tendencies of those who were struggling for independence. For most of the 1960s the MPI ascribed to an ideological platform that was approved of in 1962 and entitled *La Hora de la Independencia* (The Hour of Independence). This document was a clear expression of revolutionary nationalism. It specifically called for the "nationalization of foreign companies ... the elimination of the imported bourgeoisie ... state control of banks ... and central planning." In other words, the platform was more of a Social Christian conceptualization than a Marxist vision.[60]

The demonstrations against the Vietnam War, along with the widespread mobilization of young people in Latin America had a major radicalizing impact on all of the independence groups in Puerto Rico. At the end of the 1960s the MPI declared itself to be "anti-imperialistic and anti-colonialist." The organization declared its aspiration to create "a society with no exploitation of man by man."[61] In spite of this it did not see itself as a Marxist workers' party but rather as a national liberation movement.

---

[60] Mattos Cintrón, Puerta sin casa, 13.   [61] *Claridad*, May 5, 1968.

However, a few years later with the creation of the PSP, the organization officially adopted a Leninist philosophy and organizational model. At the Extraordinary Congress of 1974 it approved the thesis of *La Alternativa Socialista* (The Socialist Alternative) and endorsed a "program of transition to socialism."[62] This was the height of the organization's radical militancy. According to numerous testimonies from former militants, after 1974 the party slowly began to modify its revolutionary ideology for a more reformist platform. Finally in 1982 the party leadership decided to officially abandon the Marxist project. The MPI returned to its origins as a broad-based movement for national liberation.

Ideology of the CAL

Like the other armed groups, the CAL was born from the struggle for Puerto Rican independence. Its ideology was based on the ideas of some of the great nationalist leaders of Puerto Rico, including Ramon Emeterio Betances, Eugenio María de Hostos, and Pedro Albizu Campos. They emerged publicly in 1968, the year of the centennial anniversary of the Cry of Lares. In spite of its explicitly nationalist orientation, the struggle of the CAL was clearly and explicitly connected to the Marxist-inspired nationalist movements in Cuba, Algeria, and Vietnam. In one declaration it maintained:

We have always been mindful of the experiences of revolutionary struggle in other countries. For example, the Algerian experience with urban struggle is relevant, but we have to consider their example in the context of Puerto Rican reality, which has its own particular – though not exceptional – characteristics. We apply the experiences of revolutionaries everywhere in the world to Puerto Rico whenever we can ... We believe, as Che Guevara said in his message to the Tricontinental about the many Vietnams, that the most important way to lend solidarity to revolutionaries elsewhere is to develop our own struggle against Yankee imperialism and all the oppressors. We seek out the best ways to develop our own efforts, and we also rely on the experience [of revolutionaries] in different parts of the world.[63]

It is also important to note that though the CAL attacked foreign monopolies, it did not ever claim a position in favor of the socialization of the means of production. On the contrary, it defended Puerto Rican

---

[62] Partido Socialista Puertorriqueño, *La Alternativa Socialista. Tesis política* (Carolina: Impresora Nacional, 1974[a]).

[63] Cúneo Elizondo, "No somos el brazo armado de una organización determinada."

private property.[64] It *did*, however, criticize capitalist corruption, the mafia, gambling, drugs, and prostitution on the island. In terms of tactics, the organization frequently cited the examples of many armed movements that were engaged in urban guerrilla warfare:

[Urban guerrilla warfare] was used in Vietnam ... These tactics were also used in the Cuban Revolution. Anyone who has studied the war against Batista from 1956 to 1958 knows that the Cubans not only fought in the Sierra Maestra with rural guerrilla *focos*. There was a wide network operating in the cities in coordination with the command in the Sierra. The urban guerrillas made use of many hundreds of bombs, always with some explicit tactical objective. When devising a strategy – whether it is military or political – it is important to seek out a well-defined objective.[65]

Nevertheless, the CAL did not ever discard the use of other means and other political forces to fight for independence. Beal, in a public debate against the pacifist positions of the PIP stated the following:

We believe that it is indispensable for us to create a liberation army in order to achieve independence. And we will not relent in our quest to continually build a better and bigger army. The struggle will require many other things. Perhaps we will need an electoral party that has thousands of votes, or a non-electoral political movement, or both things. But those things will not be sufficient to achieve independence. There will be no freedom without a liberating army. We will take charge of building this army. We entrust others with the rest.[66]

Ideology of the PRTB-EPB – Macheteros

In the case of Macheteros, the name of the organization refers back to the independence movements of the nineteenth century. As evidenced by the other cases in this volume, naming Cold War–era revolutionary organizations for movements from an earlier era was not uncommon in Latin America. "Macheteros" makes reference to a group of rebels who participated in the wars of 1898. The term "machete" is also an allusion to the tool used by the most humble rural workers. And it is also a weapon.[67]

The ideological antecedents of the movement can be found, on the one hand, in the independence movements of Puerto Rico and of Latin America with their heroes (Simón Bolívar, Antonio Valero of Bernabé,

---

[64] See *Claridad*, February 20, 1972.   [65] *Claridad*, June 11, 1972.
[66] *Claridad*, May 16, 1971.
[67] José Torres, *Ojeda Filiberto Ríos: su propuesta, su visión* (San Juan: Ediciones Callejón, 2006), 119.

Ramón Emeterio Betances, Eugenio María de Hostos, and José Martí), combined with the influence of twentieth-century nationalists such as Pedro Albizu. But like all of the groups considered here, the ideology of the Macheteros was also strongly influenced by the Cuban Revolution and the Marxist-inspired liberation movements that were taking hold throughout the Third World.

As part of this historical legacy, combined with the goal of emancipation, Filiberto Ojeda called for the country's integration with the rest of the Caribbean islands in an Antillean Confederation. Likewise he argued that Puerto Rico should be part of Latin America. Nevertheless, on numerous occasions he defined his Macheteros as a nationalist revolutionary organization:

[We] consider ourselves to be the historical continuation of a process that began more than two centuries ago. To a certain extent, there is a thread that binds the entire history of the struggle for Puerto Rican liberation. The Boricua Popular Army – the Macheteros – are revolutionary nationalists. Our revolutionary spirit requires that our struggle for justice and social equality be enthroned in our fatherland, our national territory, our "puertorriqueñidad," and in our history of liberating struggle. Our struggle comes from the fact that we are a colonized people who have been subjected to the most violent injustices of social inequality, lack of sovereignty and lack of national freedom. And we have suffered under the boot of a foreign colonial government.[68]

Similarly the followers of Ojeda read classic works relating to Puerto Rican nationalism (Betances, Albizu, Corretjer), and other philosophers and ideologues who wrote about national liberation (Frantz Fanon, Castro, Guevara) as well as classic Marxist texts (Marx, Engels, Lenin).

The Macheteros clearly identified as revolutionary nationalists just as the other armed groups did. But all of the armed groups under discussion here, including the Macheteros clearly differentiated themselves from the reformist and pacifist groups fighting for independence:

Our current strategic conception of armed struggle is not of a "frontal" nature. Fundamentally we commit acts of armed propaganda. That is, all of our armed actions carry a clear political message about the nature and vision of our conception ... this has always been the means by which we have given armed support to the struggle. We always keep our actions consistent with the possibilities of the moment in a way that our internal development allows. For the workers ... the trajectory of the armed struggle has diverse gradations. Armed propaganda, when it carries a formative organizational political message, is the basis of all of our action during this historical stage. ... We are demonstrating that

---

[68] Declaration of Filiberto Ojeda Ríos (October 8, 2014), see *Claridad*, October 13, 2005.

our understanding of armed struggle is not a whim, not *foquista*, and in no way orientated towards terrorism.[69]

The actions of the Macheteros were limited to selective attacks on targets that represented US interests in the archipelago. Likewise their activity was integrated with labor activity and problems that affected poor communities. Through various public proclamations and documents they also consistently called for unity and the alliance between all social movements.[70]

CONCLUSIONS

This chapter has outlined some of the features of armed struggle in Puerto Rico during the period of the "new struggle for independence." With the exception of one small movement (the MAP) that briefly tried to build a foquista column in the countryside, the rest of the armed organizations in Puerto Rico were urban. From workplaces to the slums, they sought to integrate into the problems and daily struggles of the Puerto Rican citizens. The armed militants supported striking workers, war protestors and other groups that found themselves in opposition to the US presence on the island.

Armed struggle emerged and was influenced both by the international context and by the repression that the Puerto Rican people experienced during these decades, especially among those who were pro-independence.

In all of these organizations it is possible to see the legacy of the great Puerto Rican nationalists such as Ramón Betances and Pedro Albizu. And in some of the organizations we can see the clear influence of a Marxist-Leninist doctrine.

With the exception of MPI–PSP (which had both a legal and a clandestine presence), the rest of the organizations centered only on armed guerrilla actions. The Macheteros did however try to integrate into the open and legal protests of the working class and poor communities and neighborhood associations. All of these groups were actively engaged in "armed propaganda" seeking to cause property damage while avoiding casualties within the Puerto Rican population.

Even though the activity of the Macheteros continued after the many arrests during the middle of 1985, the organization was continually

---

[69] Ibid.
[70] Filiberto Ojeda Ríos, "The Boricua Popular Army-Macheteros: Origins, Program and Struggle," *Latin American Perspectives* 127 (2002): 104–116.

diminished both in terms of numbers of militants and impact throughout the second half of the 1980s and the 1990s. The assassination of Ojeda in September 2005 was a terrible blow to the organization. As for the PSP, after the internal struggles of the 1970s and 1980s, the party slowly fell apart until it was officially dissolved at the beginning of the 1990s. In spite of the fact that the armed struggle ended, numerous ex-militants continue to work for the independence of Puerto Rico. Like the militants in several of the Caribbean revolutionary movements discussed in the volume, many of these former combatants have taken up electoral politics.

Suggested Reading

Arroyo Muñoz, José Carlos. *Rebeldes al Poder Los grupos y la lucha ideológica (1959–2000)*. San Juan: Isla Negra Editores, 2003.

Corretjer, Juan Antonio. *Albizu Campos and the Ponce Massacre*. Chicago: National Committee to Free Puerto Rican Prisoners of War and Political Prisoners, 1985.

Corretjer, Juan Antonio. *Problemas de la Guerra Popular en Puerto Rico*. Ciales: Casa Corretjer, 2002.

Denis, Nelson A. *War against All Puerto Ricans: Revolution and Terror in America's Colony*. New York: Nation Books, 2016.

Duany, Jorge. *Puerto Rico: What Everyone Needs to Know*. New York: Oxford University Press, 2017.

Fernández, Ronald. *Prisoners of Colonialism: The Struggle for Justice in Puerto Rico*. Monroe, ME: Common Courage Press, 1994.

Manuel Maldonado, Denis. *Hacia una interpretación marxista de la historia de Puerto Rico y otros ensayos*. Río Piedras: Editorial Antillana, 1977.

Mari Brás, Juan. *Abriendo Caminos*. San Juan: Causa Común Independentistas, 2001.

Paralitici, José. *Sentencia impuesta: 100 años de encarcelamientos por la independencia en Puerto Rico*. San Juan: Ediciones Puerto, 2004.

Rivera, Oscar López. *Oscar López Rivera: Between Torture and Resistance*. Oakland, CA: PM Press, 2013.

Suarez, Awilda Palau. *Veinticinco años de Claridad*. Río Piedras: Editorial de la Universidad de Puerto Rico, 1992.

Websites

Puerto Rican Independence Site
   www.latinamericanstudies.org/epb-macheteros.htm
PIP
   www.independencia.net/2015-11-30-02-46-29/el-pip

Films

Filiberto 2017
I Believe in America (2007)
Las Carpetas (2012)
Machetero (2008)
Palante, Siempre Palante! The Young Lords (1996)

7

Armed Revolutionary Movements in Comparative Perspective

When Fidel Castro and his armed guerrillas launched a revolution in Cuba, they inspired a generation of young Latin Americans to seek their own revolutionary goals through armed struggle. This was especially true in the Caribbean Basin, which was home to several significant and impactful armed revolutionary movements, including the URNG in Guatemala; the FMLN in El Salvador; the FSLN in Nicaragua; the FARC, the ELN, and the M-19 in Colombia; and the MPI-PSP, the CAL, and the Macheteros in Puerto Rico. All of these movements together were important to the shape of Cold War politics in the region. These Cold War armed revolutionary movements have much in common with one another; nevertheless, they all had distinct historical trajectories and have transitioned into the post–Cold War era in different ways.

The Caribbean Basin has always held an important geopolitical position for the United States; however, during the Cold War, Cuba and its Caribbean neighbors provided the central "hot" front for this global conflict between the super powers. Of course Cuba, Guatemala, El Salvador, Nicaragua, Colombia, and Puerto Rico all had their own internal political dynamics, but the Cold War provided both financial and military resources to warring armies, and it also provided a broad ideological and geopolitical frame. The conflicts ranged from full-fledged civil wars in El Salvador and Nicaragua to intense and violent civil strife and police brutality in Puerto Rico. And the United States was both indirectly and directly involved in every one of these struggles. The United States fought the Cold War as a proxy war and as a "hot war" in the Caribbean Basin.

After the triumph of the 26th of July Movement in Cuba, the possibility of an armed struggle as a vehicle for social change and revolution became a relevant consideration for young social reformers around the world. The example of the Cuban Revolution opened up new possibilities for making revolution. Prior to the Cuban Revolution, the ideas of Karl Marx, the Bolshevik Revolution in Russia, and the Chinese Revolution all provided ideological inspiration for would-be revolutionaries in the Caribbean. But Cuba provided a relevant and a seemingly more practical model. The Cuban example seemed both more appropriate to the region and more palatable. The military phase of the Cuban Revolution lasted less than three years, and it was comparatively less costly – both in terms of human life and overall destruction – than other twentieth-century armed revolutionary movements. The publication of Che Guevara's *Guerrilla Warfare* in 1961 only confirmed and intensified this perception. Guevara emphasized the idea that poor and marginalized campesinos could be the protagonists of a socialist revolution. He also made the astonishing claim that there was no need for any kind of military or political preparation. Revolutionaries would come naturally from guerrilla warfare, and guerrilla warfare would be successful if it was undertaken with confidence in a context of extreme poverty. The example of Cuba made it seem as though revolution could be relatively quick and easy. This proved to be irresistibly enticing for a generation of young people who hoped to enact social change.

In addition to structure, mobilization strategy, and ideology, the five cases here can be compared in terms of their historical trajectories and their impacts on the national political and social climates. The similarities between the experiences of all of these movements are numerous, and interrelated. In all of the countries, the impetus for armed rebellion was primarily a nationalist one, especially in Puerto Rico and Nicaragua. In addition to their opposition to US hegemony and imperialism, guerrillas in all five countries were responding to gross social inequalities and historical injustice. They were all in the midst of significant economic transformation (modernization toward an export-based economy and nascent globalization). In all five cases, these primarily nationalist movements were transformed by the context of the Cold War and quickly adapted to it by adopting a range of Marxist ideologies, which mostly proved to be inflexible and ultimately divisive.

INTERNAL STRUCTURES

As military organizations, all of the guerrilla movements in this study had a common vertical hierarchy. In every country discussed here guerrilla insurgencies that followed the success of the 26th of July Movement and the publication of Che Guevara's *Guerrilla Warfare* were heavily influenced by the Cuban example. For the armed revolutionary movements in Guatemala, Nicaragua, and Colombia, Guevara's explanation of the guerrilla *foco* in Cuba was a particularly compelling example. Consequently they initially tried to adapt this foco strategy to their own national circumstances. The fascination with *foquismo* led to loosely and tenuously organized guerrilla organizations in those countries in the early 1960s. Foco theory ultimately proved to be unworkable in the countries where it was attempted. It led to devastating consequences in most cases.

Although the Cuban Revolution and the success of foquismo in Cuba also influenced Puerto Rico, it did not pursue the rural strategy (with one brief and unsuccessful exception in an organization called MAP). Puerto Rico's already well-developed independence movement adapted to armed revolutionary struggle after 1959; while it was influenced by the Cuban Revolution, it was undertaking an actual anti-colonialist movement (rather than a metaphorical one) and literally sought to be liberated from protectorate status *vis-à-vis* the United States. This movement was fundamentally an urban one, and it was tied to long-standing and legal political parties on the island.

El Salvador is the other case where the influence of foquismo was minimal. Because of the historic strength and influence of the Salvadoran Communist Party, El Salvador was discouraged by the Soviet Union from pursuing an armed strategy in the 1960s. The Salvadoran Communists continued to maintain strong ties to the Soviet Union throughout the 1960s, and the Soviets were generally opposed to Cuban-style revolutionary movements and guerrilla warfare. Consequently armed revolutionary struggle did not fully emerge until the 1970s, by which time foquismo had become discredited.

During the second decade of struggle, most of these armed movements had explicitly abandoned the foco approach, and they all worked more diligently on forging political and social relationships with a larger constituent base. Some of the organizations experimented with Leninist democratic centralism as an organizational model, but the reality of guerrilla warfare made this less influential than it might have been otherwise. Ethnic realities were different in all five countries; this coupled with geographic differences explains the various ways in which the movements sought to build a broader base of support. Some of the organizations had been decimated by the US-backed counterinsurgency campaigns of the 1960s, and some groups were left more intact. But all of the groups that are under study here emerged with a larger geographic base of operations in the 1970s, and a broader commitment to establishing widespread support among multiple sectors within their own national contexts. This commitment to broadening their bases influenced the evolution of the structures of the armed movements.

By the late 1970s and early 1980s, most of the guerrilla movements in the region (with the exception of the Puerto Rican case) had undertaken the task of creating umbrella organizations or other strategic alliances. In Guatemala the URNG became the united guerrilla organization. In El Salvador the FMLN represented all the guerrilla factions. Nicaragua had the FSLN. And Colombia – for a time – had the CGSB. In the Central American cases these umbrella organizations were more successful than in other Latin American countries, and these new alliances formed the basis for negotiated settlements and future political parties.

MOBILIZATION STRATEGIES

Like the internal structures of these movements, the mobilization strategies of the organizations that adapted foquismo (in Guatemala, Nicaragua, and to some extent in Colombia) were influenced by the Cuban example. In the early to mid-1960s many working class and middle-class guerrilla leaders launched their movements in isolated rural areas and attempted to recruit campesinos and campesino families to their cause. This strategy proved to be disastrous in many cases. The guerrillas had only a limited knowledge of the terrain where their movements were based. And the communities that were supposed to provide logistical support, and where the armed revolutionaries hoped to mobilize new recruits, became vulnerable targets for devastating attacks by the national armed forces. In all of these cases, the armed revolutionary movements began to adopt a range of other mobilization strategies and actively sought to recruit a broader range of militants from different social sectors by the late 1960s.

All of the cases here, including Puerto Rico, experimented with a range of mobilization strategies in the 1970s. While the question of whom to recruit and how to mobilize them was never definitively settled, by the end of the Cold War era all of the remaining organizations understood the need for developing a political base that would be broad and diverse enough to support the transition to a competitive political party in a post-conflict era.

IDEOLOGIES

In all of the countries studied here, the traditional communist parties acted as a conservative influence. The country with the most established communist party – El Salvador – delayed the initiation of a serious armed rebellion for almost a decade. Even for the countries where the communist party had not deeply penetrated, socialist ideology was influential. The Cuban Revolution and the Cold War context meant that these nationalist movements that were initiated as a response to the profound social and economic inequalities of the region were highly incentivized to see their struggles in the larger geopolitical context of the Cold War. Even if they had not found Marxist ideology to provide a compelling remedy for economic injustice (which was being exacerbated by the global capitalism), US military support for zealous *anti*-communist regimes made it impossible for these movements to ignore the ideological dichotomy presented by the Cold War.

Having said this, Latin American Marxism was often rooted in a commitment to democratic socialism. The guerrilla organizations during this period were uniformly nationalist. Their commitment to Marxist-Leninist-Maoist principles was often tenuous, and the ideologies of the organizations evolved considerably over time.

Moreover, the United States was heavily involved in designing and supporting counterinsurgency efforts, particularly during the Reagan years. The brutal counterinsurgency campaigns of the national governments in the countries where the guerrillas operated exacted enormous human costs, but they also prompted the growth of the human rights movement that eventually pushed armed revolutionary movements toward more respect for liberal democracy and the rule of law (and away from the more dogmatic adherence to Marxism).

Some of the organizations under study here were more closely tied than others to nonviolent popular movements. The FMLN, the FSLN, and the Puerto Rican independence movement all had strong ties to a range of other social movements. The level of popular mobilization was higher in the more densely populated and more ethnically homogenous countries such as El Salvador, Nicaragua, and Puerto Rico. But even in Guatemala and Colombia the connections between the armed movements and "the people" ebbed and flowed over time. Ideology was tied to the relationship between the guerrillas and the people in many ways and was influenced by the social movements with which the guerrilla organizations affiliated.

HISTORICAL TIME FRAME AND LONGEVITY

All of the countries already had well-established reform movements and/ or significant social conflict *before* the Cuban Revolution. Guatemala's liberal reform government was overthrown in a CIA-sponsored coup, and the possibility of rectifying the social and economic injustices caused by US economic dominance and anti-communist paranoia seemed to be intractable to peaceful popular intervention by 1960. In El Salvador campesinos and workers had decades of experience with social resistance and mobilization. Nicaragua's relationship with the United States was the most similar to Cuba's; by 1960 Nicaragua had been run by a US-backed military dictator for decades. Government repression of any and all opposition was becoming more intense and more explicitly linked to the anti-communist rhetoric of the United States. Colombia also had been consistently embroiled in violence, almost since its independence from Spain in the early nineteenth century. And Puerto Rican activists had been organizing to seek independence from the United States since the 1930s.

None of these armed revolutionary movements came to the decision to wage guerrilla warfare in a historical vacuum. The most devastating and long-lasting of the Cold War confrontations in the region played out in the countries that were already embroiled in civil conflict. Colombia, which had not even emerged from the civil war known as "La Violencia," is the best example of this. Although the first Cold War armed group (the FARC) did not officially declare itself until 1965, it came directly out of the campesino self-defense groups that had been allied with the Colombian Communist Party since the late 1940s. After the emergence of the FARC and the ELN in 1965, a Cold War frame was put on top of the existing social and political conflict. In Guatemala – a country that had experienced the foreign usurpation of its democratic reform movement – underwent a failed attempt at a *coup d'état* by a group of military officers in November 1960, which led to the first guerrilla actions of the MR-13 during the early months of 1961. The MPI-PSP (in Puerto Rico) formed in 1959 as a political movement, but it recognized from the outset that armed struggle might be required. Most scholars believe that there was some sort of armed clandestine movement in Nicaragua after the death of the elder General Somoza in 1956, and that this nucleus eventually led to the formation of the FSLN in 1962. And in Puerto Rico both the CAL and the Macheteros (which emerged formally at the end of the 1960s) had their origins in other independence movements that were allied with the Cubans after 1959. The leaders of the Salvadoran Communist Party broke away from the party by 1970 to launch armed movements. The M-19 (which formed in 1972 in Colombia) was completely constrained by the polemical and virulent Cold War politics of the time.

The transition *away from* armed struggle also came in stages. The Colombian movements were the first to engage in negotiations with the government. And the M-19 was the first guerrilla organization to make the transition to a political party. Ironically the FARC is the most recent case of this transition, and the ELN (also in Colombia) has yet to sign a peace accord with the government.

After coming to power through an armed insurrection in 1979 in Nicaragua, the FSLN was immediately transformed into a ruling political party with Daniel Ortega at its head. Ortega stepped down (from the presidency) in 1990 after losing an election to Violeta Chamorro and her UNO coalition. In 2007 Ortega once again assumed power (representing the FSLN) after winning the presidential elections in 2006. Since that time Ortega has worked to change the Nicaraguan Constitution, and the FSLN-controlled government has eliminated term limits, allowing Ortega to run for office every five years indefinitely. Ortega's ruling coalition has also sought to eliminate the main opposition parties, making the FSLN's current commitment to the principles of electoral democracy questionable.

The FMLN finalized a peace accord with the Salvadoran government in 1992 and has operated as a political party ever since. The president of El Salvador in 2018, Salvador Sánchez Cerén, represents the FMLN and is also a former FMLN commander. The URNG made the successful transition to electoral politics in 1998 (after signing accords with the Guatemalan government in 1996). Despite this, its influence as a political party has been minimal, especially as compared to that of the FMLN and the FSLN. And in Puerto Rico, the MPI-PSP, the CAL, and the Macheteros all gave up armed struggle by the late 1980s, although some Puerto Ricans (and former militants of the armed struggle) still continue to advocate for independence through other means.

IMPACT

In the years immediately following the end of the Cold War and throughout the 1990s, mostly conservative governments with a neoliberal agenda were in power in most of the region. Neoliberalism is an economic ideology sometimes associated with globalization. The main policy elements of neoliberalism in Latin America are (1) the promotion of international trade; (2) increasing foreign capital investment by incentivizing the potential rewards; (3) privatizing the economy by selling off publicly owned property (e.g., public utilities, subsoil rights, transportation infrastructure, and public health and education infrastructure); and (4) deregulation. Because these neoliberal policies are dependent upon the increasingly globalized international economy, opposition to these policies is often conflated with anti-globalization efforts. Eventually the economic repercussions of these neoliberal economic policies led to economic crises (most significantly in Argentina in 2001), popular unrest, and the emergence of New Social Movements.

New Social Movements (NSM) emerged in Latin America after the end of the Cold War and have been distinguished by their expansion of political identities beyond class-based analyses, as well as their opposition to neoliberal economic policies. These new movements have been organized around more complex social identifies such as race, ethnicity, gender, and sexuality. They also abandoned the goal of taking power from the state and instead have focused on more specific issues or problems, often related to neoliberal policies. The rise of these New Social Movements coincides with a pendulum swing to the left that had begun by the turn of the century. This leftist trajectory has sometimes been referred to as the "red tide," or the "pink tide," and was epitomized by Hugo Chávez's "Bolivarian Revolution" in Venezuela and the Zapatista uprising in Mexico.

Hugo Chávez led an unsuccessful coup attempt against the government of Venezuela in 1992, in an effort to overthrow the government of Carlos Andres Pérez and his neoliberal policies. After Chávez was released from prison, he founded a political organization called the "Fifth Republic Movement"[1]; through this new populist coalition, he was elected as president of Venezuela in 1998, 2000, 2006, and again in 2012. He was never inaugurated for his fourth term in office, however, because he died of cancer before he could assume the office again. Chávez's Bolivarian Revolution[2] was a continental political movement that was committed to undoing the neoliberal policies from the previous era, redistributive socialism, and its hostile posture toward the United States. Bolivarianism (both in Venezuela and elsewhere in Latin America as it was promoted

---

[1] *Movimiento Quinto República*

[2] The reference to Simon Bolívar highlights the pan-American solidarity that was crucial to the movement. Simon Bolívar, the father of independence for the northern countries of South America, was known for his pan-American sentiments and ambitions. He envisioned a "United States of Latin America" that would counter the power and influence of the North.

by Chávez) was highly nationalistic and represented a kind of democratic socialism that was reminiscent of the ideological traditions of the revolutionary armed movements that are the subject of this text. Chávez implemented a state-led economy in Venezuela without abolishing private property, and he heavily emphasized both national autonomy (especially from the United States) as well as pan-Americanist solidarity between Latin American nations. Many Latin Americans saw Chávez's populism and his Bolivarian "brand" to be attractive. And there were Bolivarian allies, including some former Cold War–era guerrillas, elected to governments all over the region in the early part of this century.

In Mexico, the Zapatista National Liberation Army (EZLN)[3] was the first post–Cold War guerrilla movement. Although it was founded as traditional Cold War–era guerrilla organization in 1983, it did not emerge publicly until January 1, 1994, after the Cold War had ended. The Zapatistas were opposed to the implementation of the NAFTA accords (which were indicative of the neoliberal policies of the era) in Mexico. Although it refrained from military action after January 1994, it maintained its posture as an "army." It is significant as an armed "revolutionary" group that was representative of the anti-neoliberalism movement. And it has remained active and influential as a New Social Movement. What most distinguishes the EZLN is that it has never sought to overthrow the government, or to take power. In 2016 it reversed its long-standing policy of rejecting electoral politics and promulgated a candidate, María de Jesús Patricio Martínez, who will participate in the 2018 presidential elections. Patricio Martínez is an indigenous woman, and she will be the first female indigenous candidate for the presidency in Mexican history.

The protagonists of the armed revolutionary movements from the Cold War era were also involved in this pendulum swing to the left. In El Salvador, Mauricio Funes of the FMLN political party was elected as president in 2009. And while Funes was never an active militant guerrilla in the FMLN, his successor in 2014, Salvador Sánchez, was a former military commander of the FMLN. The FMLN is effectively the ruling party in El Salvador. Likewise, Daniel Ortega and the FSLN are firmly in control of the power structure in today's Nicaragua. In both of these countries (despite the somewhat anti-democratic tendencies of Ortega and the FSLN) they rule their countries from a fairly moderate democratic socialist position. The legacy of the armed revolutionary movements in those countries is clear.

[3] *Ejército Zapatista de Liberación Nacional*

The URNG in Guatemala has been less successful in electoral politics. Already by the mid-1980s, the FMLN was a more democratic political organization than the URNG. The FMLN more fully embraced the transition to electoral politics much earlier than did the URNG, and the URNG also entered into negotiations with less military strength than did the FMLN. Both organizations have had some electoral successes, but the FMLN has unquestionably been the more successful of the two parties. The racism and ethnic divisions in Guatemala have also muted the long-term impact of Cold War revolutionary politics and the URNG. Virulent racism and the history of ethnic oppression in Guatemala exacerbated the historical injustices there. State terrorism devolved into genocide during the Efraín Ríos Montt dictatorship in Guatemala. Racism also infected the armed revolutionary movements, particularly in the first phase. Racism and racial divisions also complicated the peace process as well as the transition in Guatemala.

In Puerto Rico today, there are still remnants of the independence movements of the twentieth century, although they do not have much popular support (especially as compared to the movement that advocates for statehood).[4] The debt crisis and the long-term effects of Hurricane Maria will make the dream of an independent Puerto Rico even more untenable going forward.

Colombia is now finishing the transition away from the Cold War. It remains to be seen how post-conflict Colombia will fare. Popular support for the FARC has waned in the past decades, and a substantial political minority still opposes the peace between the state and the FARC. Still, Colombians have learned from the experiences of the Unión Patriótica in the 1980s, and the M-19 in the 1990s, as it has learned from its Central American neighbors. Peace will ultimately depend upon local communities. And the ideals of the armed revolutionary movements from the 1960s may eventually find inclusion in the political dialogue, but it is still too early to know what this might look like.

Social justice advocates and New Social Movements can learn from these experiences. Dogmatism and ideological rigidity are harmful, but so are sectarian differences based on identity categories. Charismatic leadership is perhaps important in the Latin American context, but flexible and enduring horizontal organization is equally important. Armed insurrection seems imprudent and unlikely in the current political context, but it is

---

[4] In a status referendum in 2012, only 5.5 percent voted for independence, while 61.1 percent of the votes went for statehood.

still important to be able to threaten the entrenched power structure somehow. It is also important to note that the armed revolutionary movements of this era in the Caribbean Basin were overwhelmingly male. This was not always the case with armed guerrilla movements elsewhere in Latin America.[5] Despite the fact that women were militants and even leaders in almost every guerrilla organization, and despite some minimal acknowledgment of the societal oppressions of women by some of these movements, most of the organizations discussed here were not particularly supportive of women leaders; there is evidence of sexism and misogyny in many of these organizations. A commitment to human rights for all and the rule of law continues to be key to the future of New Social Movements and social justice. The armed revolutionary struggle for change during the 1960s, 1970s, and 1980s included both successes and failures. While the armed struggle may be over, the story of the quest for peace and social justice is clearly not finished.

---

[5] Guerrilla organizations in the Southern Cone were, in some cases, fairly evenly split between male and female militants.

Index